REMEMBERING LEE

Recollections of Lee Lozowick by Students and Friends

Edited by Regina Sara Ryan

HOHM PRESS
Chino Valley, Arizona

ADVANCE PRAISE FOR *REMEMBERING LEE*

This compendium of stories and anecdotes is a beautiful way for us to continue partaking in Lee Lozowick's living presence. The most mundane circumstances of everyday life are the very space where the teacher's basic goodness is revealed, as well as his insight and his sacrifice for the good of others, in other words, his relentless efforts to help each person become more transparent to the divine.—**Eric Edelmann**, spiritual teacher, writer in the Vedanta lineage of Swâmi Prajnânpad and Arnaud Desjardins. Director, Mangalam Ashram, Québec

The delightful stories in *Remembering Lee* display the relationship between a true teacher and a true student. When these two come together, the student goes through radical transformation and spiritual development ensues. Readers will taste this nectar, and their own path will be enhanced.—**Lama Palden Drolma**, meditation teacher and counselor, author of *Love On Every Breath*

Lee was an impeccable warrior, always putting the dharma, the Work first, before himself, before his own comfort, before his suffering to an extent which is nearly unbearable for our ordinary level. He left such a strong imprint on all those who met him that he still deeply inspires our daily life.—**Veronique Desjardins**, teacher, Hauteville Ashram, France

Lee's memory comes alive through all these short stories. I loved reading it! In reading his journal once, and now again with this book, I am left with such a strong impression of how much he was loving, caring, and dedicated to every one of his students, serving the highest possibility for each of them.—**Sophie Edelmann**, teacher, Mangalam Ashram, Canada

Remembering Lee is a fitting tribute to Mr. Lee. Over the three decades that I was privileged to periodically meet him, in various contexts and locations, I regularly witnessed first-hand how his teachings shaped lives, and how sincere was his concern for the spiritual well-being of those he taught. These individual testimonies of interactions with him form a worthy homage to a relentless, quixotic guide whose life bore witness to the transforming power of the love of God.—**Dr. Robert Svoboda**, Ayurvedic physician, and author of 12 books on the sciences of India.

Cover Design: Hohm Press
Cover illustration: Zafreen Zerilli

Interior Design and Layout: Becky Fulker, Kubera Book Design, Prescott, Arizona

Library of Congress Control Number: 2024931190

ISBN: 978-1-942493-92-1
e-book: 978-1-942493-93-8

Hohm Press
P.O. Box 4410
Chino Valley, AZ 86323
800-381-2700
http://www.hohmpress.com

This book was printed in the U.S.A. on recycled, acid-free paper using soy ink.

With Gratitude and *Jai Guru!* to Lee Lozowick

&

In Loving Memory of Sita Martin

CONTENTS

Foreword ix
Eric Edelmann

Editor's Introduction xi
Regina Sara Ryan

The Remembrances 1
Students and Friends

Afterword 159
Rick Lewis

About Hohm Press and Contact Information 166

FOREWORD

It is a joy and also a great honor to be able to write a few words of introduction for this book dedicated to the remarkable Western spiritual master Lee Lozowick. I had the privilege of meeting him on many occasions between 1992 and 2010. The fact that he was also a dear friend of my own master Arnaud Desjardins certainly helped me appreciate Lee for his true value. Appearances are indeed misleading—one had to refrain from being put off by his attire or some of his deliberately provocative assertions, as his intention was always to shake us out of our grossest identifications.

Arnaud himself admitted that there was at times something "mysterious and unfathomable" about Lee but nevertheless he held him as the greatest disciple of his own master, Swâmi Prajnânpad, even though Lee belonged to a completely different lineage. I didn't always understand the purpose behind his actions, which in a way reminds me of this remark by the wife of Albert Einstein : "I don't know anything about the theory of special relativity, but I do know my husband and I know he's right!" I fully trusted Lee's clarity of vision, his integrity, dedication to his disciples and, above all, his heartrending devotion to Yogi Ramsuratkumar, the yogi saint of Tiruvannamalai. I am not surprised that, during his funeral, a multitude of rainbows filled the sky throughout the day, suggesting that he was on very good terms with celestial beings and other deities.

I have often been dazzled by the depth of his knowledge in the spiritual domain and his ability to articulate for us—often with humour and incisiveness—the countless biases and pitfalls that stand in the way of sincere seekers on the path. He was indeed vast enough to effortlessly adapt to a line of teaching that was not his own, and impeccably answer the questions of Arnaud's students, most of whom he was meeting for the first time.

When he generously accepted our request to host retreats in Quebec on a regular basis, I was able to witness, among other things, the full magnitude of service that he manifested. In many ways, Lee remains an inexhaustible source of inspiration for me. I must admit I deeply loved this man; he touched my heart from the first moment I met him.

It seems to me that this compendium of stories and anecdotes is a beautiful way for us to continue partaking in his living presence. The most mundane circumstances of everyday life are the very space where the teacher's basic goodness is revealed, as well as his insight and his sacrifice for the good of others, in other words, his relentless efforts to help each person become more transparent to the divine.

This collection of testimonies, most of which are shared by his close students—may they be thanked here—allows us to appreciate how a genuinely spiritual life can illuminate the day-to-day lives of others. Uncompromising obedience to the Will of God is not a reality lost in ethereal mysticism. It is a powerful force, an energy of which Lee was the vehicle. This book offers a magnificent illustration thereof and it will contribute to nurture our gratitude, always and forever.

—Eric Edelmann, spiritual teacher, writer in the Vedanta lineage of Swâmi Prajnânpad and Arnaud Desjardins. Director, Mangalam Ashram, Québec.

EDITOR'S INTRODUCTION

The many individuals who have contributed to this book have had one thing in common. Each one has met (in person or in dreams) and spent time with (sometimes hours, sometimes decades) the American-born spiritual teacher, Lee Lozowick (1943-2010). This is not a chronological collection, nor a compilation of dharmic teachings. It is rather a testimony to a human being who devoted his full adult life to the benefit of others. Not necessarily to their worldly accomplishments—although he was a passionate advocate for our success in various arts, be they aesthetic, healing or humanistic, and even our business ventures—but primarily to the realization of our true nature, the possibility of surrender to and love for God, and the liberation from the prison of our limitations.

"He always had my well-being at heart," said one student of Lee's, "whether I agreed with his direction or not, whether I currently 'liked' him or not. I cannot doubt that he was committed to my highest potential."

Many words and phrases have been used to describe this man Lee—including "Indian saint," as applied by his own spiritual master, Yogi Ramsuratkumar, the beggar-saint of Tiruvannamalai, South India; "Anjenaya," a name for the deity Hanuman who was ever faithful to his beloved Lord Rama; and "Khépa," which means "mad for the Divine." Some descriptors indicated Lee's fierceness with ego, which constantly reared its head among us. Others captured his crazy-wisdom approach or demeanor in everything from his mode of dress (in wearing used items picked out of a recycled clothing bin) to his rock n' roll persona, so lavishly and arrogantly displayed as a singer in his rock bands (LGB or *liars, gods and beggars* and his European group, the *Lee Lozowick Project*), along with his blues band (SHRI). They referred to his uncompromising and often loudly enunciated stand for the purity of the teaching, especially within the coterie of new-age wannabe-yogis and yoginis, whose empty promises filled the spiritual magazines of his day and attracted thousands of gullible seekers to their programs.

The reader here will find less of the fierce and more of the simply kind. Less of the crazy and more of the shockingly generous. Less of the uncompromising and more of the quietly surrendered Lee. This book is a tapestry of sorts, a patchwork jacket, full of the many different colors that this wisdom teacher, Lee, wore and shared. Never a mountain-top guru, Lee as a teacher was always immediately and enthusiastically involved in the lives of each of his students. And, because many of these stories have come from an individual's personal exchange with him, it is deliciously spiced with secrets, some of which even his closest students may be surprised to discover. It is also full of tried and true *lilas*, some of which have been repeated and enhanced over decades to new people and old standbys alike. Taken together, they create an intimate display of an extraordinary ordinary man. A man who, in his own words, wanted to be remembered as one who "made us laugh."

The book was conceived and begun in 2001 by Sita Martin, one of Lee's close students, who handed out small yellow legal pads one day to anyone willing to start collecting or remembering their *lilas* with Lee. The word "lila" is a common Sanskrit term used in many contexts, essentially meaning "play" and often linked with the word "Divine," as in "the play of God." Lilas are also applied to short teaching lessons or stories collected about the life and work of a teacher or guru. The telling of lilas is a favorite pastime of devotees, who seem to never tire of recalling their love for the master or teacher. In the *Bhagavata Purana*, which recounts the love-games, or love-play, of the divine incarnation, Lord Krishna, it is reported that the *gopis* and *gopas* (cowherders and milkmaids, his earliest disciples) rekindled their joy and bliss in him by telling stories of his exploits with them, long after he had departed their company to carry on further work for creation.

This too was Sita's intention, and one to which she was dedicated. It was for her a heart-work. Her death in 2004 brought the project to a halt, and it took years to track down the original notes, which fortunately had been preserved. It took further years to complete the culling process that has resulted in the book you now hold. Like Sita, who was a dear friend, sister and mentor in so many ways, I wanted reflections and remembrances that reflected on Lee more than on "me." The writing of a lila can easily devolve into a demonstration of how *small* the student is by comparison with how *great* the teacher was—a common error among starstruck Westerners new to a path or tradition. And in 2001, many of the people represented in this book were still in their prime! Many of us, fascinated with our new-found path, our amazing teacher, our radical community life, told our stories of what Lee did or said heavily weighted by our own views and projections and interpretations. For me, some of these stories held a sense of their usefulness to others in the future, particularly for those who had not known Lee; while other lilas, not so. Consequently, dozens of these original remembrances, as touching as they were, didn't make the cut for this volume.

I have been helped by a team of dedicated readers who further reviewed the lot, offering their insight and suggestions.

I am indebted particularly to Mary Angelon Young, Lee's biographer, along with RedHawk, Tom Lennon, Bhadra Mitchell, Elyse April, Peter Cohen and Nancy Lewis for their valuable assistance in this project. The remembrances you have before you were initially intended to number hundreds more, but the work involved was too extensive to accomplish within my foreseeable lifetime. I have thus been inspired by the two recent publications, *Zen Is Here*, and *Zen Is Now,* edited by David Chadwick, about his teacher Suzuki Roshi, which are each small in page count, but highly evocative in content. It is my sincere wish that further collections may follow, if readers find this one to be of value. In the meantime, you are recommended to a four-volume *Study Manual*, also published by Hohm Press, as well as three volumes of Lee's biography, *Spiritual Slavery* by M. Young.[1]

And, on that note, careful readers who met or knew Lee will likely be reminded of many other moments that demonstrate the vast rainbow of his being. Please send your stories to Hohm Press, and either I or my associates will save them for future publication. I love the fact that so many of us were entrusted with such secrets—teachings that were given to us alone in a particular time and place, and which are now able to be revealed for the universal context they point to. It is time to share them.

—Regina Sara Ryan

1 *Hohm Sahaj Mandir Study Manual*, volumes I-IV, Hohm Press: Chino Valley, Arizona, 2002, and *Spiritual Slavery: A Biography of Lee Lozowick: The Years of Milk and Honey, 1975-1980*, Hohm Press: Chino Valley, Arizona, 2011. www.hohmpress.com

THE REMEMBRANCES

A Siddha

A Tibetan master told our group that there were two kinds of sages, a *mukta* and a *siddha*.[2] A *mukta* teaches in a very straightforward way—easy to understand. While with the *siddha*, you never know what they will say or do. Often you cannot understand them when they speak.

"At last," I thought when I heard this, "now *that's* a definition of *my* guru!"

2 By definition: mukta (मुक्त) refers *to "liberation,"* according to the 11th century Jñānārṇava, a treatise on Jain Yoga in roughly 2200 Sanskrit verses. *Siddha* (Sanskrit: सिद्ध *siddha*; "perfected one") is a term that is used widely in Indian religions and culture. It means "one who is accomplished."

A Flower for Mother

When my son was three years old, my wife and I brought him to Sunday night *darshan*. He was curiously walking around the space during the chanting and offerings of *prasad*.[3] At one point he walked up to Lee's dais and reached out to touch the flowers that had been given to Lee. Seeing my son's interest in them, Lee spoke gently: "Take one flower and give it to your mother. She deserves one." My son then carefully took one flower and toddled back to bring it to his mother.

3 From the Sanskrit root "to see," *Darshan* is the sighting or seeing of a deity or revered person. Lee held a Sunday evening program every week in which we joined for chanting and an exchange of gifts (*prasad*). He would speak and answer questions during this meeting. We referred to the gathering simply as "Darshan." Prasad would be offered to Lee, usually fruits or flowers or candy, and Lee would return a gift to the devotee, usually a piece of candy or other sweet.

Thrilled by the Storm

In the summer of 1976, at his old center in New Jersey,[4] Lee and another man were outside in back of the house when a huge crash of thunder rattled the building. Moments later the rain and hail moved in, coming down in torrents against the roof and walls. I was seated inside with a view to the back door when it flung open at the same instant that a big flash of lightning illuminated the sky and the electricity in the building went out with a sizzle. Lee was at the back door, and as he entered and closed the door behind him, the lights came on again.

He was ecstatic! In fact, I remember that he was gleefully clapping his hands together. Wide-eyed and joyous, he blurted out, "Wow! It's really exciting out there." He could hardly contain the pure energy of the whole experience.

A few moments later, the door flew open again, and the male devotee who had been outside with Lee came in, drenched from the rain. "Oh, God," he yelled, "it's terrible out there. Terrible. I'm soaked to the bone and it's going to take me hours to dry off. Why the hell do we have to live here in New Jersey anyway?"

Lee calmly looked up and replied, "Well, why not?"

The man was speechless. He paused silently for a long time, and then, reconsidering Lee's words, he quietly stepped back outside into the pouring rain. Lee and I stayed at the window for a long time, just enjoying the wondrous explosion of nature.

---

[4] A house that became Lee's first official center where students worked and gathered for programs.

1 Broken Foot, 3 Teaching Lessons

In 1993, during a trip with Lee and company in Europe, I broke my foot and needed to navigate on crutches. One morning, when the rest of the group was at breakfast and I was alone in the dorm where all the women were staying, Lee came in and asked me if he could use my crutches. "Of course," I replied, wondering *what on earth*? Soon, he was hobbling and stumbling about in the room. At one point he placed one crutch down and played with using the other one like a rifle. "Bang," he cried, as if shooting something. *My ego?* I wondered.

A few days later I was with the group on the second floor of the building when Lee announced that he and another man were going to carry me down the stairs. I was a bit embarrassed but had learned enough not to reject the guru's offerings. They carried me down.

Later in the week, I slowly started out on foot (with crutches) towards the location where Lee was to meet a famous Zen teacher. By the time the group caught up with me I was nearly exhausted, and hot. Taking off my heavy coat I asked my companions if someone would carry my coat. Before anyone could respond, Lee immediately took the coat and carried it for the rest of the afternoon.

Emptiness Is Form

Three years after joining Lee's community in 1985, I had the privilege of accompanying him on a trip to Europe. One evening, just prior to a talk he was to give in Munich, he sat in the front seat of the van while one of the women in his household combed his hair and fastened it into a ponytail at the back of his head.

The scene was such a simple one, and the hair-combing such an ordinary gesture, yet it was filled with the greatest tenderness and devotion, and I felt honored to be witnessing it. Although I had only been around for a few years, I had noted that the spiritual master was generally embarrassed by outward displays of affection, so one rarely had the opportunity to see him in such an intimate (although natural and commonplace) situation.

As I watched, I observed that he was more than a passive participant in this process. He was, in my view, so surrendered that he literally disappeared, and for the first time since entering the school I was gifted with "seeing" him. I stared at his form, but I was staring into infinite space, and this seeing left me breathless, as if I was standing on the edge of an abyss about to jump.

From that day until now, although decades have intervened, I have never forgotten this revelation of Emptiness, and have only to remind myself of its reality to both see and feel it again.

Committed 100 Percent

I first met Lee through friends in California who frequently hosted him there, and I was regularly invited to gatherings, talks, and meals. We spoke briefly of my Zen teacher, Joshu Sasaki Roshi, for whom Lee had great respect. When I was able to visit the Prescott ashram in 2009, I attended an evening talk and darshan there. Lee's voice was almost gone at this time, due to throat cancer, and one of the women close to him was repeating his words.[5]

At one point, he was berating one of his students for not reaching out to him in the midst of a difficult situation that she was going through. He bristled with a fierce compassion as he said, "How can I help you if you won't let me know what is going on?" I got to see that Lee's commitment to his students was 100 percent.

Years later, I was reminded of Lee when my teacher, on the occasion of celebrating his 52nd anniversary of coming to the U.S., surveyed all the ordained and committed students gathered there and told us, "You are not prepared for how much you will love your students and disciples."

---

[5] Lee was diagnosed with cancer in 2007 and died in 2010.

Making a Profit

Sometime before 2007 I had arrived at the ashram in France[6] with great anticipation in seeing Lee again, but when I entered the room where he was working, he didn't look at or acknowledge me in any way. I had expected that at least he would stand up and say *something* as he usually did. But no. Instead, when he finally caught my eye, he pointed to a painting he had recently acquired in his art and bronze business.

"Do you want to buy this picture?" he asked, quite matter-of-factly.

Honestly, I had no relationship to this type of art, and was not at all attracted to the particular picture. But, at the same time, I sensed that "something else is going on." Such was almost always the case around the spiritual master. I knew that his direct question to me was an invitation of some sort.

"Yes," I replied. "I'll take it." Immediately I could see that I had said what he wanted to hear. His delight was obvious, but still he had not acknowledged me personally.

A short time later, I overheard him in conversation with a woman who had also recently arrived. She was inquiring about the painting that I had purchased, still on the table near Lee's desk. "Was it available?" she wanted to know. But Lee's reply was strong, "No, it is his," he said, pointing toward me.

Then, the most remarkable thing occurred. I had this strange sense that the whole interaction around the picture was a particular dance between the master and myself. I felt

6 La Ferme de Jutreau, Lee's ashram in central France near the city of Poitier.

acknowledged and connected to him. "It's only about 'us.'" I thought to myself.

But Lee wasn't finished with this play yet. Turning to the woman he said, "You can only have this picture if you are willing to pay him two times the amount he paid me." To my utter amazement the woman was untroubled by this arrangement. "I will," she said, without hesitation, and she did!

Lee was delighted. I watched him, seeing in him the mood of a young child. Beautiful.

He really caught me! And I know it brought me close to him. Even today, many years later, I'm still shivering in my heart just thinking about this.

The Smell of Cigarettes

I was driving Lee from Paris to Frankfurt, which required an all-night push, and I was growing tired. This was a very hard assignment, and I was on edge that I might fall asleep. At some point, when exhaustion had almost overtaken me, I thought that I could clearly detect the aroma of Indian cigarettes. Lee's master, Yogi Ramsuratkumar, regularly smoked Charimar-brand, and used these cigarettes, or so it was believed, as a means of smoking away the karma of whomever was in his presence.

Lee was awake, and I asked him directly: "Do you smell the cigarettes of Yogi Ramsuratkumar?"

"Yes," he answered, with intensity.

I had no more difficulty in continuing the journey from that point on, as hard as it was. I realized that I would not have to be in the Yogi's physical presence to get his transmission. If I was open to him, I would receive his grace anywhere, anytime.

A Gift

I wanted a conch shell to use for our pujas and asked Lee if he had any in the Sacred Bazaar.[7]

Apparently, these shells were in short supply at the time, so the likelihood that I would have one was rare. One day, shortly after my request, as he explored the antique and specialty shops in the city we were travelling through, he came upon a rare collection of the precious conches, and Lee bought them all. That same day, calling me aside, he asked me which one I favored, and when I picked it out, he graciously handed it to me.

"This is a gift," he said, smiling.

---

7 The Sacred Bazaar was Lee's name for his business of selling sacred artifacts from many different countries and traditions. He sold at his ashrams, and carried his artifacts with him on speaking engagements. He had several galleries in which this art was sold both in France and the U.S.

Trust?

On a Sunday night in the early 1980s, we were all sitting in darshan with Lee when one senior student, a man, asked him a question about trust, and what it meant to follow the teacher's word without hesitation. After a brief silence, Lee looked quickly about the room like a cat about to pounce on its prey. "Okay, why doesn't everybody take their clothes off?" he said.

Instantly, the whole room froze, except for the one man who had asked the question. He leapt to his feet and started peeling his shirt over his head like crazy, while the rest of us sat there like chunks of granite. I was petrified. A lot of jaws dropped in disbelief. A few people tried to ask a question, stalling for clarification, "You mean . . . like now? Here?" But the words couldn't form properly.

After four or five seconds, Lee blurted out, "Okay okay okay okay!" The instruction now canceled, the senior man disappointedly but with good humor donned his shirt and sat down. Lee then regaled us for nearly an hour about how our stated and impassioned desire to serve did not necessarily give us the strength to break through the unwillingness we had exhibited only a few moments before.

His Surrendered Concern

In June of 1988, in Munich, Germany, our group had accompanied Lee to hear a rock band in a small club off one of the narrow side streets that form a labyrinth in the heart of town. The vans had been parked a significant distance from the club, and by the time we walked there after the performance I observed that one of the women in our party was missing. When word began to spread about her absence, I watched the various reactions of our group to the event—from concern, to guilt to annoyance. When I looked at Lee, however, he seemed unperturbed. He was simply present, aware of the situation.

"Let's just wait here while somebody walks back to get her," was his gentle remark. I recall thinking that he was simply trusting this woman's maturity to be able to care for herself, with whatever was up.

A short time later, the scouting party returned with the missing person, and we piled in the van wordlessly. Lee drove. No further comment was ever made.

A Train Ride from Hell

In December 1993, we were on our way to Anandashram in Kerala, India,[8] by train. It was an all-night trip. When we boarded the train there was barely room to stand with our luggage. I was very depressed about the prospect of standing all night. Eventually, I got a seat on a wooden bench with others and could observe Lee who was on a similar bench two rows down from me.

All night, I struggled to get comfortable and sleep a little bit. My position changed constantly: sitting straight, then slouching, then bending forward. I hated being there, intensely. Occasionally, I glanced over at Lee. He was sitting straight up, the whole night, his eyes closed, apparently relaxed, with his hands unmoving and folded in his lap. He never moved once, as far as I could tell.

---

8 Anandashram is the ashram founded by Swami Papa Ramdas, who was the guru of Yogi Ramsuratkumar.

Amateur!

It was June 1987, and we were boarding the Paris Metro for our last train trip at the end of a band tour with Lee.[9] We pushed our way through the open doors into the overcrowded train car, grasping whatever available handholds were near. The whistle blew and the doors closed.

Suddenly, Lee's voice clearly and distinctly cried out, in French, "*Amateur amateur*!" He was looking directly at two young Parisians. He had managed to catch hold of one man's hand that was attempting to slip into his open pocket. Lee had what I'd call "a shit-eating grin" on his face and seemed to enjoy the interaction. In order to complete the interchange between himself and the pickpocket, Lee reached deep into the same pocket which the man had hoped to violate and pulled out an old, scrunched up tissue which had scribblings from a devotee on it. He offered it to the embarrassed young man, all the while with an expression of humor, delight, and genuine humility on his face. Neither this man nor his companion knew quite how to respond to Lee's spontaneity and stood there looking rather dazed and confused. Lee turned his head in our direction and let out a laugh.

The train soon came to a stop and the doors opened. The two young men scurried out as quickly as possible never once looking back.

---

9 Lee's bands toured through Europe (and continental U.S.) for nearly two decades. Along with the musicians and vocalists, dozens of his students from many countries participated in these experiments, providing lots of inconvenience, joy, and practical work-on-self for all involved.

As we completed our train ride, I found myself nostalgically recalling the stories I've read of Lord Krishna and his worldly adventures, where Krishna had quickly outwitted any tricks or treachery attempted on him by his many enemies. Lee seemed to enjoy turning the tables in a somewhat gentle, sometimes not so gentle, manner.

What Happened?

In the early 1990s, I sat near Lee on a train outside of Paris enroute to a seminar program he was giving. A young girl child was laughing with her mother and dancing around in the empty space by her seat. I noted how absorbed Lee was in his attention to this child who was so spontaneous in her actions.

Later that day, during one of his talks, Lee told the story of this little child's behavior on the train. Many of us had witnessed her delightful show along with Lee's interest in it.

"Seeing the mood of that child," Lee said softly, "you should all have been asking yourselves, 'What happened to *me*?'"

Jealousy

During a band tour, we were off the road for a few days at La Ferme de Jutreau (Lee's French ashram), sitting outside in a circle on the lawn, discussing something with Lee and about twenty other band members and students. For weeks, and throughout our many gigs, I had been beleaguered with jealously, and now I desperately wanted to just leave and go home.

"I can't do it," I said to Lee and my companions, referring to my struggles, which were obviously having an effect on others. Several people in the group nodded their heads in agreement, ready to let me go. I couldn't blame them. It had been brutal.

Lee didn't hesitate. "Well, if you *can't* do it…" he said.

As he spoke those words, looking at me, I found myself in a tunnel, my entire field of vision was rapidly closing in on me, going to black, with only the tiniest speck of light remaining. The words that came out of my mouth in that moment, however, were surprising: "I *don't know how* to do it!"

"Oh, well, *that's* different," Lee immediately responded.

Instantly, the interior tunnel and darkness receded for me, bringing the light back again. Once again I found myself sitting in a circle surrounded by the sunny warmth of the summer afternoon.

A short while later, I was standing in the doorway to the main house, Lee close by. He turned to me and said, "Once I smashed a dent in the dashboard of my Porsche."

"Because you were jealous?" I queried.

"Of course," Lee replied, "what else?"

A Room at the Inn

I was having a difficult time throughout one of our extended band tours with Lee's first rock band, LGB (*liars, gods and beggars*). I was a single man, hoping to meet a woman, and very horny! The longer the trip went on, the worse it got. Finally, I went to Lee one night to complain of several things and tell him how sexually frustrated I was.

We were staying in a somewhat meagre accommodation, which was par for the course on tour, and were packed several guys to a room. Lee, however, had a room of his own, as we always arranged it for him. On this particular night, after my complaining and just before we went on stage, Lee took me aside. He told me that if I found a desirable woman at the gig that night, I could invite her to spend the night; he would give me his private room and sleep with the other guys!

Shocked, but so touched by his generous and unexpected offer, I don't remember what I said. Probably just an incredulous "thank you."

I didn't take him up on the offer. I wasn't willing to venture out of my own comfort zone to take such a risk. Too bad, I reflected, years and years later, realizing that he was giving me a chance to break free of my own tight little world.

A Message to Never Forget

Once, in 1984, I was so frustrated at one of my coworkers in our ashram business that I went to Lee in utter desperation, unable to figure out any way to work with them. Minutes later, after I had finished expressing my whining, helpless attitude, he approached and gave me a scrap of paper. On it, he had written, "Instead of thinking why it can't be done, think of ways to do it."

Ten years later that same scrap of paper serves as my bookmark in Lee's books of poems to Yogi Ramsuratkumar.[10] Since I read a poem every day, I have a daily reminder of his gift.

---

10 Lee wrote hundreds of devotional poems to his spiritual Father, Yogi Ramsuratkumar. They have been collected in three volumes: *Death of a Dishonest Man, Gasping for Air in a Vacuum, and Intimate Secrets of a True Heart Son,* all published by Hohm Press.

A Look of Love

At Lee's request I was translating a letter he had received from a French woman who had been at his seminar in Paris a few weeks before. She had been profoundly touched, and described sitting in the dark, two days after meeting him, crying and calling out for him. She felt scared of the intensity of her new feelings, yet deeply in love. I raised my eyes from the letter feeling that same sorrow, love and longing. It was the type of love that breaks your heart yet enlarges it a hundredfold. Wondering if I was going to start to cry right there in front of my beloved guru, I looked at him and saw that he had tears in his eyes.

A Clear Compliment

While I was completing some duties in Lee's kitchen, he passed through and started to rant and rave about the behavior of another devotee. His seemingly bitter tirade was painfully hard to digest, for me, and without a thought I blurted out, "Baba, please, I don't want to hear it."

He stopped near the stairway, turned to me with an ear-to-ear grin and twinkling eyes and said, "Great work." Then he proceeded down the stairs.

A Teaching for Life

As a person who is always moving, always on the go, I have received many teaching lessons from Lee that have affected me strongly. Perhaps one of the strongest, however, occurred in 1992 while I was in the midst of acting out my usual unconscious and habitual means of working and dealing with my life. On that day, Lee turned to me and said, "Don't just do something, stand there."

Working Outside the Box

I had just completed carefully packing (I thought) two boxes of books that were to be shipped from the ashram, when Lee entered the office. He took one look at the boxes, which were on the floor, and began jumping up and down on one of them. As he did so, he ranted about this inept job of packing and how they would probably be destroyed in the post.

I was shocked! I don't know if I said anything in the moment, but I did notice that suddenly my breathing changed, radically. Instead of being constricted, I was actually breathing freely, which is rare for me as I am prone to severe allergies.

Lee then walked to his desk and resumed his work, reminding me casually to check the other box. I did so, and with a similar fervor *I jumped on it* . . . and it easily opened at the seams.

Looking up, Lee caught my eye. We both laughed.

No Gift Wasted

Early spring, 1993. For years I had kept an old, brightly-colored dress-robe that had been a favorite of mine as a devotee of another master. It was one I had worn at this master's ashram for special events, darshans and celebrations. Now, having found myself in the company of Lee, and very grateful, I still had a hard time parting with this item of clothing, although I knew I would never wear it here, as it was still too encoded with my previous life experience. So, what to do with it? I couldn't bring myself to burn it in a *yajna* fire—a ceremonial cleansing fire that we held periodically on the ashram—as I still hoped it would have some use to someone.

When the Bauls visited our ashram in '93,[11] I had the idea to give it to them, since they make their clothing out of patchwork collected from many sources. Although I tried several times, waiting for the right moment, it didn't happen. I even tried to send it to India with a group that was going to Bengal, but no one would carry it. So, there it sat in my closet becoming more and more of an invitation, but to what?

At last, not knowing what else to do, I gave it to Lee one night in darshan. Then, I breathed a sigh of relief; at last, it was gone and I thought no more about it.

---

11 The Bauls are an iconoclastic sect of poets, singers and dancers who express their longing for God through their art. They beg their subsistence through their arts. At Lee's invitation, several Bauls, including the respected guru, Sanatan Das, visited Prescott in 1993 and did a performance tour of the Western U.S. which Lee's students arranged.

A few weeks later, working in Lee's kitchen as the Tavern server,[12] he came in dressed for the evening, and occupied himself arranging some food on a tray. Two members of his household were also in the kitchen and they coyly inquired how I liked Baba's new Tavern pants. "Do you recognize them?" they asked, gleefully.

"No," I admitted, somewhat puzzled by the odd question. "I have never seen them before." Still, they insisted that I did.

I started to wonder if I had recently put anything into the giveaway box in the ashram greenhouse, where we left our recycled clothing, and which Lee regularly explored for his "wardrobe" needs. Then, it hit me. There was my old ceremonial robe, now transformed. Lee had asked one of the women to make it into a pair of Tavern pants for him.

To this day I am so moved by the recollections of his little actions that let us know how deeply he understood and informed our lives. Through his grace, although its form had changed, my old robe still made it to darshan.

12 The Tavern was the late-night gathering space, a specially-decorated room in which Lee met with devotees every night to share tea, sweets or nuts, and quiet good company. The name evolves from the Tavern of Ruin of Sufi lore in which the lovers of God gather to share their longing for the Beloved. The Beloved's glance or presence is referred to as a "wine," which causes the most sublime intoxication. Hence, the descriptor "Tavern."

Darshan in the Garden

I would be unable to attend darshan on a Sunday night because I needed to drive one of our sangha sisters to the Phoenix airport.[13] Together, we went out to the garden to find Lee with the news that we were leaving. In our good-byes, I mentioned that this would be the first time in two years that I had not attended a formal darshan since moving to the ashram. I was feeling somewhat sad about that. Smiling gently, looking at me, Lee said, "Then we can just have darshan in the garden." And in that moment, we did.

13 *Sangha* is a Sanskrit term referring to the association or group of devotees or practitioners following a similar path.

Any Picture You Want

One night in May 1994, shortly after Lee had sent the huge statue of Avalokiteshwara, the bodhisattva[14] of compassion, to the Sonoma Mountain Zen Center of Jakusho Kwong-roshi in California, I noticed that the photograph of this deity had disappeared from the wall in the dining room and asked Lee if it was removed because we should not be attached to "her."

"No," he said, "one of my students had mentioned that he wanted a photo of the bodhisattva, so I gave it to him."

He then asked if I wanted one of the pictures on the wall. "Go ahead and pick one," he said.

I pointed to one. "No," he responded. "That's a photo, pick a picture."

I chose a Middle Eastern collage of images that I often looked at during our meals. Lee immediately took it off the wall and handed it to me. "It was painted by a friend of my father's," he said as he handed it to me.

Such generosity. And such surprises.

---

14 This was a fourteen-foot-tall artifact that had been given to Lee by friends in New England. It had once belonged to Swami Rudrananda. When it was brought to the Prescott ashram it was too tall for the Darshan Hall, so the roof was raised to accommodate it. After living with us for many years, Lee sent the bodhisattva as a gift to the Sonoma Mountain Zen Center, where it resides today.

A Gift of Touch

During a SHRI gig[15] in April 1994, the place was very crowded. At the break, people were moving around quite a lot. I was sitting at one of the few tables with my body turned around to talk to a friend. Someone bumped into my crossed legs as they moved past me and I immediately (and somewhat neurotically) blurted out "I'm sorry," excusing myself for the fact that *my* legs were in the way!

I looked up to see that it was Lee! Our eyes met, gently. I realized my common neurotic responses, along with the unusual circumstance, simultaneously.

Lee reached down and gently touched my leg, with a short stroke actually, and excused himself for knocking into me. The touch of his hand, and the touch of his eyes . . . I will not soon forget that healing moment.

---

15 SHRI was Lee's blues band and longest enduring music project which continued after his death. Lee was the lyricist and a singer for the band until 2010.

Innocent Purses and Whimsical Socks

Lee loved to shop, and he especially loved getting a bargain. He also delighted in giving gifts, which many of us received spontaneously over the years. One day, he came back from a huge garage sale in town. He carried in box after box of his purchases and set them in the office. Another woman and I were terribly curious as to what he had bought and what he was so excited about. As he opened one box, we saw that it contained nothing but second-hand purses—old purses, vinyl handbags, obviously cheap knockoffs. I thought they were the ugliest purses I'd ever seen, even as he beamed with joy saying, "I thought some of the women might be able to use them."

My companion and I exchanged glances of horrified delight! His joy was utterly innocent—he imagined that these would be great treasures for us. How could we refuse? So, we gratefully accepted, while suggesting that the children would probably love to have a bunch of them for their dress-up collection.

The next box contained socks—the biggest, thickest socks I had ever seen! Knowing what my shoes and boots could bear, I immediately realized that they would be useless in such cases. Without comment, Lee gaily handed each of us a pair, along with several additional pairs to distribute to other people. Then he left the room, and my companion and I couldn't stop laughing. The beauty of his innocence and his whimsy raised our spirits to a fever pitch, and we held our bellies as the peals of laughter didn't stop.

Those socks, worn inside the house on cold winter nights, kept our feet warm for many years to come.

No One

I saw something one morning that I'd never seen before. More accurately, I saw nothing. As we stood by my car, one minute I was looking into Lee's eyes and they were full of a familiar twinkle, richness. Then they changed from a deep well of emotion to nothing. I looked deeper and realized there was no one there! All the while Lee was looking at me, straight through me, it seemed, and yet I didn't feel like someone was looking at me.

I couldn't hold onto a gaze like that. It was like looking into the sky or into the ocean. Even more so, like looking into nothingness. Then I got frightened, and I felt Lee's gaze quietly comforting me. I reached out and grabbed his arm, as I wanted to be reassured that he was still actually there.

I was immediately embarrassed and disappointed in myself because of my frightened reaction. Seeing Lee as nothing, as no one, was startling, and it still is. I'd been gifted with a glimpse of Reality.

Relentless Love

Lee was relentless in continuing his work with a woman devotee who was dying on our ashram, while at the same time instructing us serve her in every way we could. She didn't have long to be here, to work with him, and he didn't give in to any sentimentality or pity for one moment with her. Many of her caregivers honestly found him somewhat harsh.

Only days before she died, she had a resurgence of a desire for life. She began to eat and drink again, which she had not done for several days, and which had greatly relieved her pain. She asked to be carried outside. She attended the Sunday darshan and teaching meeting held every Sunday morning and was carried around the property on her litter, even sunbathing. But, with this new lease on life came a return of her agonizing pain.

At an after-dinner-talk[16] in which she was not present, one of the care team asked Lee about her apparent change in outlook. He responded, genuinely emphatic, if somewhat enigmatically, "Sure, let her have anything she wants. She was just this close [he moved two fingers together almost touching] from the arms of the Beloved. If she chooses to turn her back on it and return to this vale of tears, then let's give her all the help she wants. She can have watermelon and even strawberries out of season. Give her anything she wants!"

[continued]

16 Lee would give talks and answer questions on Tuesday and Thursday nights after dinner, usually for two hours. These gatherings of the sangha were known as "after-dinner-talks."

He was impeccable and relentless where ego was concerned. No one was spared, no matter their condition or pain. There was nowhere we could go—or a stage we could get ourselves into—in which he was not there, working with us.

No Defense

I had asked for a "work task," and Lee recommended that I be observe silence for six weeks. One afternoon during that time, I was in the office when a small indiscretion on my part triggered a huge verbal outpouring from him. In so many words he had nailed my ego's strategies, and in front of a group of others. I couldn't speak a word in my own defense...which is probably a great blessing! I felt humiliated, embarrassed.

When it was over, I retreated to the case temple,[17] apparently to go back to work, but more to cry my eyes out and lick my wounds. Sitting outside at one of the worktables, sobbing, I noticed Lee approach. He hardly *ever* visited the case temple unless he had specific business. But there he stood, not looking at me or anyone, but furiously working the mala beads[18] in his hands.

Was it just a coincidence that he was there, close to me, at a time when I needed help or consolation? Maybe. Nonetheless, a new wave of tears arose from me, but these were for the compassion I felt from him.

---

17 The "case temple" was a basement garage that opened out into the yard, and in which the ashram's glass-case construction business was housed. Individuals worked here as service to help support the community financially, and Lee himself would sometimes be found there.

18 Mala beads are prayer beads used to count the repetition of a sacred *mantra or nama,* the name of God.

No Sins Here

Repeatedly I observed that whatever "sins" I was internally berating myself for, and often the uglier I felt about myself, the more warmly, openly and happily Lee greeted me. Once, when I first met him, I had written a letter to him in which I declared my shortcomings. He wrote back that he would never single me out for my "imagined sins," adding, "I simply view you differently."

Flying Pancakes

After our Fry Bread Booth project[19] ended one summer, we had a full bucket of dough left over. Rather than throw it out, in accordance with Lee's wishes to use up leftovers whenever possible, one of the cooks took a courageous leap to salvage it. She made pancakes.

It sounded like a great idea. We even had a special breakfast the next morning at Arrakis[20] and lots of people came from town. It looked like a great meal, and the smell of fresh pancakes drifted all through the office and made everyone hungry by the time we all sat down.

Unfortunately, the dough was three days old, and had already gone completely flat so that even prodigious amounts of butter, honey, grape jam, and real maple syrup couldn't disguise the fact that they were all as tough as leather. Many could not even be cut with a fork. Some were as hard as a rock. I think I ate three, just on principle, and mostly tore them with my hands. Yet, in the midst of harsh grumblings of disappointment, characterized by an occasional "Oh my god, can I borrow your knife?" Or, "Can you please cut this into pieces for me?"

[continued]

---

19 The Fry Bread Booth was a Hohm Community project that took place on the Prescott town square every year during the July 4th rodeo week. For decades, we served up frybread with many different toppings to hundreds of tourists and locals alike. It was a major source of income for the ashram.

20 Arrakis was the name of the main building on the Prescott ashram. It included offices, the Darshan Hall, a dining room used every Tuesday and Thursday, a kitchen and Lee's residence.

everyone had their token pancake or two, with a sense of humor. It was like a crazy experiment that failed miserably and became so laughable in its absurdity that the food became secondary to our just being together.

Meanwhile, as everyone was finishing up what little they did manage to eat, the cook and I were in the kitchen gaping at the mountains of uneaten pancakes that were still waiting to be served. Lee came in just then with an armful of pancakes from the dining room. He then yelled out exuberantly, while calling out our names: "Look, pancakes!" and whoosh, began tossing them across the room like frisbees. They zipped right between us and bounced off the window and onto the floor with a series of loud thuds, leaving all of us in such laughter that we practically fell on the floor.

No One To Be Offended

Lee once criticized my approach to my work, as well as my general attitude towards him. At first, I recoiled and argued that his remarks were unfounded. Then to defend myself further, I claimed that my shortcomings "really weren't so bad." But, as Lee held firm, I recognized what he was pointing to and had to admit that he was right. On the spot I apologized and asked him to forgive me.

"There is no such thing as forgiveness," Lee replied.

He went on: "When one is disposed in a certain way, there can be no offense taken. There is no one to be offended. And since there is no offense, forgiveness is impossible."

A Radical Space Change

I first met Lee on September 1, 1985, at a conference in Sacramento, California, hosted by E.J. Gold.[21] The night before the event and into the morning I felt powerful resistance to attending this conference. It was like a storm was whipping through me. Still lying in bed, the storm passed and an incredible calm came over me.

Next morning, arriving at the site, I found out that no arrangements for childcare had been arranged, so my daughter would have to stay with me, limiting my access to the talks. When word got out that Lee Lozowick was coming, my husband wanted me to see him. "It would be good for you to stick around," he said.

I went to the program and watched Lee enter with a group of women, all dressed in white. He was very soft-spoken, I remember. When EJ left the room, many others departed, but Lee stayed and began talking to those around him. That's when I felt a radical space change. He calmly stood there talking about . . . *sex*! But I wasn't hearing that. I was hearing something very different. I was drawn to his eyes, and I connected to him.

He looked back, directly at me. I was struggling to hear what he was saying, while also trying to quiet this busy child in my arms, and further seeking to discover what "the Work" is, as he was describing it. With that look, I knew he understood. . .all of it.

I knew I would look for him again.

---

21 E.J. Gold is a Fourth-Way teacher and was a friend of Lee's for many decades. Lee visited EJ frequently at his home in northern California.

He Turned Them Away

It was a hot summer evening in the early 1980s when I first met Lee at a public darshan in L.A. I had been going to the local study group there, led by one of Lee's earliest students. I had heard many stories about Lee, so I was quite anxious to meet him in person. Lee was in rare form that night. He had just returned from India and was throwing pieces of bread all around the room after prasad had been given out. He was making all kinds of sexist remarks. At times, he was insulting to people in the audience, and then in the next moment kind and genuine. All throughout, I found him to be funny. He was laughing most of the evening. A lot of the people in the audience were totally turned off. Some even left.

While his remarks often made me feel uncomfortable, I sensed that it was all an act, and that Lee was just putting on a show. I remember asking myself, "Who *is* this guy? *This* is a spiritual master?"

I left that evening with no insights or inspirations. Nothing I heard struck a chord with me. Based on what he said, coupled with his antics, I could see nothing special. However, I felt a strong connection and sensed a kindness and sincerity in him that really spoke to me. It was not an intellectual connection, but one of feeling: a connection with my heart and what I felt and saw in his eyes. It was this connection that kept me coming back for more, and finally brought me home...Hohm (the name of Lee's community).

A Volunteer

At a Tuesday night dinner on the ashram in April of 1994, I announced that I needed a volunteer to accompany me to Scottsdale the next day. I was giving a talk and needed someone to sell books at the end of the presentation.

One woman responded that she could *possibly* help, but she would need to re-arrange her schedule and it might not work out. I again looked down the table to see if anyone else would volunteer, since I needed a definite commitment. Silence. No more offerings.

Just then, Lee spoke up: "If she can't do it, I will go." My heart jumped at his generosity. "After all," he looked directly at me with the innocence and sincerity of a child, "I have nothing better to do."

It was clear to me, beyond doubt, that he meant exactly that. He had nothing better to do than to support and serve his devotees constantly, which he did.

Bail-bond Buddha

One evening, Lee was playing Bridge with some students when the phone rang.[22] A new student, who had been living on the ashram for a couple of months, had been caught in town in the midst of a misdemeanor and taken to jail. The students in the room with Lee were horrified and became indignant when they learned what had happened. The consensus was that the offender should be left in jail so he would "learn his lesson." Lee, however, found the situation very funny. Not only did the absurdity of this man ending up in jail strike his fancy, but the righteous attitude of the other students seemed to tickle him as well. He reached into this pocket and casually pulled out the bail money. Handing it to one of the men in the group he said: "Tell him he's lucky I'm his spiritual master and not one of you guys." To my knowledge the student was never verbally reprimanded for his infraction.

22 Lee encouraged his students to play Bridge, the card game, as a practice. It was used as a means of self-observation and for what it teaches about paying attention and the value of cooperation with one's partner.

"Please Allow Me To Introduce Myself"

Holding back a heavy, red velvet curtain, I entered the Tavern for the first time. Lee looked at me and gestured toward a seat in his circle, across from him. I'd just seen him for the first time in darshan an hour before, and this was the moment of meeting face-to-face. The conversation flowed easily, and I enjoyed his ordinary, easy demeanor—even though his presence was anything but ordinary! At one point he invited me to come back to Prescott the next week. "We're having a celebration,"[23] he explained, "and our rock band is going to play. You might enjoy it."

My curiosity was piqued, and I returned the next Saturday with a sense of high adventure. Sure enough, that night LGB (the Living God Blues band, I was informed by eager students) performed at an old warehouse in Prescott. Along with others, I worked up a light sweat dancing, even though the band was new and we smiled at how rough the music was.

Then, I heard the familiar strains of an old Rolling Stones' song, "Sympathy for the Devil." To my great delight, Lee was singing the lyrics as if he had written them himself. Even singing off-key, he brought the song to life! Here was a real person who was comfortable with paradox, the play of dark and light.

I'd never been interested in a guru wearing white robes, advocating purity, acting holier-than-thou. This guy was different, and I was intrigued. Yes, here was a guru I could relate to, heart and soul.

---

[23] Every year the Hohm Community has celebrated Guru Purnima, a traditional holiday honoring the guru, held during the first full moon of July.

A Mother's Love

I knew I needed to see a psychotherapist, and Lee advised that he would find one for me, so just to wait. A few days later, he told me he had found a therapist and that I should start with her after my upcoming trip to Europe, but not before. Despite the warning, and wanting to simply *meet* this woman to make me feel less afraid, I went ahead and arranged a meeting with her anyway. The therapist made a favorable impression, and I was intent on following up with her when I returned.

While away in Europe, I had met Mrs. Irina Tweedie, a remarkable Sufi master, whom Lee greatly respected. Near the end of my stay, I called the ashram to tell Lee that I was returning. His response was cold and unfriendly. He had learned of my inquiry with the therapist before my trip.

"You disobeyed," he said. "For now, don't return to the ashram, so stay in England and do whatever Mrs. Tweedie tells you to do. Or come back to the states and live in Boulder and do therapy there."

Shocked, upset and angry, I slid to the floor shaking. "I will stay," I gasped. And I did, embarking on a six-month adventure that I might never have taken. I hung out with Mrs. Tweedie, who was living in London at the time. When I told her my story, she welcomed me warmly and laughed saying, "All my students are in therapy, and if not, it's because they are therapists themselves." She then gave me the number of one of her therapist-students to speak with.

Mrs. Tweedie was the most loving mother that one could imagine. At the end of six months, when I told her I was returning to the U.S. and that I was afraid, she asked me, "Is Lee really so harsh with you, my dear?"

"Yes," I said, bursting into tears.

Then she sat up very straight and said, "Then you should consider yourself very blessed."

As I left, she added, "I will pray for you, and for Lee, and for your community."

The Rock Star on the Cover

On the way to Los Angeles for a band gig with LGB, a sangha member was reading the latest issue of the community journal, *Divine Slave Gita*. As we pulled up to the inspection station at the California state line, a young guard leaned into Lee's window and asked, as usual, "Where are you coming from?"

"Prescott," Lee answered.

"Are you carrying any fruits or plants?" But then, seeming to ignore Lee's answer of "No," he noticed Lee's picture on the front of the journal that the devotee was reading. With amazement he looked at the cover, then looked back at Lee, then at the cover again: "Hey," he said, "you are on the cover of this magazine!" He was full of enthusiasm with this discovery, again saying, "Isn't that you? Let me see it. No really, I won't keep it."

The devotee handed the magazine to the guard who took it in his outstretched hand. Immediately, Lee called back to someone else in the van, "Do we have a band tape?"

The guard was now fully absorbed in leafing through the whole magazine, page after page. I recall that he even tried to pronounce the name of the magazine a couple of times. Just then, Lee handed an LGB cassette tape to him.

"What's this?" the man asked in all sincerity.

"A rock band," said Lee.

"What kind of music is this?" the guard asked again, apparently not believing what Lee had told him.

"We're a rock band," Lee said.

"No kidding?" said the guard, and again, "Really, no kidding?"

[continued]

Then the young man turned to the box on the table behind him and grabbed a stack of *Golden State* magazines, which he pushed through the window into Lee's hands. He wanted to do something, anything, to express his amazement and appreciation.

Lee and the rest of us burst into delighted laughter at the man's offering and took the whole stack.

"Be nice to the guys in the van behind us," Lee said to the man, with a smile. "They're the band too!"

As we pulled away, still laughing, I could see how pleased Lee was by the exchange. "He'll probably keep those guys a half hour talking about music," he said, chuckling.

I looked back to see the other van parked at the checkpoint, and a broad grin on the driver's face.

Just Stop It

One of my more bizarre, personal manifestations has been a tendency to grimace. I was unconscious of how much I walked around all day with my brow creased like the carvings on Mount Rushmore. Although Lee had pointed this out to me on numerous occasions and I had worked with it, or so I thought, to the best of my ability, I never *really* got it until I walked into the office one day and got the shock I needed.

There, on the bulletin board, in Lee's own handwriting, in four-inch-high capital letters, was a sign: STOP. JUST STOP KNITTING YOUR BROW.

Bridge Is Fun . . . *Not!*

Lee is a fast Bridge player. He seems to be able to memorize every move that happens in the game and therefore knows what is in your hand. As I play with him, I become extremely nervous. My mind turns to jelly, and I make many more stupid mistakes than I ever do when playing with sangha friends. This has been a constant source of frustration for me, and I assume for him, as I keep making the same errors over and over.

Sometimes he is stern with me, almost harsh. Other times he is playful and gentle. One day in 1994, early in my "career" with him, I was so upset during a game that I began to cry as I played my hand.

"Isn't it amazing," he remarked softly to the player on his right, "people forget that this is only a game. It is supposed to be fun!"

Without another word he continued his play.

"You've Never Felt It"

After years of tortured Bridge playing, I was still no better at it. In fact, I was ready to quit playing forever, convinced that I was hopeless. At the ashram of Arnaud Desjardins—a much-respected French spiritual teacher and friend of Lee's—after a particularly painful game with Lee and some of our company, I was again distraught. As we left for dinner with Arnaud, Lee took me aside and kindly suggested that I ask Arnaud about how to work with my emotions around this game.

Arnaud responded immediately to me. After telling me that he wasn't much of a Bridge player himself, and didn't particularly like the game, he shocked me by saying that I had never really felt the depth of the emotions that arose for me in this game situation. He then went on to instruct me in how to work in this way.

Lee's intervention in this case came through another's instruction that was extraordinarily effective. I *didn't* become a better Bridge player, at least not right away, but with Arnaud's help, at Lee's direction, I had a key for using my emotions and for overcoming my resistance and fear of the game.

Refuge

During the early 1990s I travelled to India and Europe with Lee, acted on stage with him, played rock and roll music all over the country in his band, led a study group in Florida, and shared other exciting and mundane adventures with his community. I bathed in the Ganges with him, bowed before his teacher, Yogi Ramsuratkumar, played music on the streets of New Orleans, sat naked with him in hot springs, and partied wild with him and a bunch of Fourth Way students. Mostly though, it was just seeing him in his magnificent ordinariness that was most striking. His form changed but his devotion to us, his students, was constant. The ashram is still my home; the sangha is my family; the master is my refuge.

Richard Baker-roshi

Lee joined Richard Baker-roshi in a café near the Sorbonne on a rainy afternoon in May 1993. The Zen Buddhist teacher had just given a public lecture which Lee and a dozen of his students had attended. As we sat huddled together at the tiny café tables, we sipped coffee or tea. Lee too drank coffee, uncharacteristically, since he had abstained from caffeine throughout this trip.

As the two men swapped amenities and stories, Lee's gaze was gently and resolutely fixed on Roshi. For years Lee had expressed to us his deep regard for this controversial teacher, and I was left with the impression that Lee was "drinking him in," absorbing from the other whatever was useful for his own work and teaching. Richard Baker, meantime, fingered his prayer beads through the entire meeting.

At the conclusion of their time together, Baker-roshi rose and graciously bowed to Lee, who reciprocated. When he was gone, Lee, in one smooth gesture, reached across the table and picked up Richard Baker's coffee cup, which was left half finished. In one quick move he drank the coffee down to the dregs. Replacing the cup, he picked up his shoulder bag, turned to the rest of us, and simply said, "Let's go!"

Tough-Love Guru

Perhaps the toughest conversation Lee and I ever had was about love. The conversation had a predictable and easy-to-learn script. In fact, I learned my lines long before I ever came into Lee's physical company. My part went like this: "I am not lovable." Lee's part, too, was always the same: "Yes, you are." The tough-love message he continued to give me, as trite as it may sound, was that not only am I lovable, but that he, himself, loved me. He was not interested at all in my insecurities, excuses, complaints or doubts; Lee's faith in me and love for me shone like an unwavering beacon of truth that left no room for old messages of self-hatred. Yes, Lee Lozowick was a tough-love guru all right!

Bodhisattva on the Phone

Lee was speaking to someone on the phone, but I only caught the last part of the sentence, which I will never forget: "Be ready to dispel your illusions with more Influence[24] direct from the heart of God."

[24] Divine Influence was one of initial and foundational principles of Lee's teaching. Namely, that the blessing force of the Divine was available and at play in every event of our lives.

Kiwi Kindness

In June 1992, Lee was having breakfast in the household of the German sangha, near the end of a tour with his rock band. The mood was quiet, reserved. I had already eaten some fruit for my meal and was halfway through consuming a slice of watermelon when I spied Lee coming through the crowd carrying a bunch of grapes and a kiwi (one of my favorite treats). Within me, a greedy voice arose, "Maybe he will give some of his fruit to me," as he often generously shared so much with his devotees. But immediately my superego voice responded, "Be quiet, you already have plenty of breakfast. Just forget it."

At precisely that point Lee passed me, as I was seated on the floor among fifteen others. But to my surprise he turned on his heel, looked down directly at me, and said, "Like a kiwi?"

Yes, I blurted out, with watermelon seeds still in my mouth. Lee then dropped the kiwi into my hand, turned and walked on.

No Wasted Tears

Lee had given me a writing task to do. When I handed it in he called to inform me that it was not useful to him, as I had not followed his directions exactly. Learning this news, I was upset, embarrassed and sad. But his words that followed were full of kindness, "Don't cry about it," he said, "and just keep moving ahead."

Just Serving Lunch

One afternoon a number of us had gathered upstairs in Lee's living room for a meeting initiated by one his students to discuss some aspect of our teaching. We had been in session for a short time when Lee entered the room and, with sparkling eyes, looked at all of us and said, "You stay right here and continue your meeting and I'll make lunch!"

Lee moved happily about the kitchen with a dish towel tucked into his shorts. We could hear him, now opening the fridge, next busily chopping at the counter. Finally, he called us to lunch and we all took our places at a beautifully-set table. On each plate were luscious, fat sandwiches with ingredients Lee had magically produced from a rather bare fridge—eggs, avocado, alfalfa sprouts, a few olives, sunflower seeds, mayonnaise, and so on, on whole wheat bread. We all moaned with pleasure as we took our first bites; the food seemed so alive, so full of life force. Lee beamed at us approvingly. We all suddenly noticed that at his place was simply one green apple and several dried figs. Lee was having his usual lunch.

The lunch was consumed all too quickly. As we finished, Lee leaned back from the table and patting his full stomach said, "Mmm, that was delicious."

Moving In

In 1990 I was living a short distance from the Prescott ashram with my wife who was, on this day, serving as the Darshan Hall attendant, spending twenty-four hours in that space, holding the intention for those who attended the November Celebration. She needed some things brought to her and I was walking through the ashram office carrying a pillow and blanket. Lee was at this desk and as he looked at me and my strange load, I quipped, "Well, enough is enough, I'm moving in." Lee's response was immediate, not joking at all, but suffused with great tenderness. "Well, you are welcome," he said.

Interesting for me that almost thirty years later, and after Lee's death, my wife and I were approved to be among the caretakers of Lee's residence, Leela Mandir, in Paulden. He had been dead over eight years, but, moving in at last, I felt that same welcome.

Watching Him Pack

Watching Lee when he packed the books to send to the Prison Library Project was always fascinating to me.[26] There were often a pile of various-sized books but no one box would adequately hold them, so the box would have to be trimmed to fit. Lee worked with such intensity and intention: no hesitation, no wasted movements. He actually turned book packaging into an art. He did this with just about everything.

[26] Founded in 1989, The Prison Library Project, initiated and directed by Rick Moore, and located with a bookstore in Claremont, California, collects and sends books to inmates in state and federal penitentiaries throughout the U.S.

Always Serving

In the last year of Lee's visits to Hauteville,[25] 2010, he was not to eat because he had cancer of the mouth and tongue. Still, he sat with Arnaud and a few other guests at the daily meals. Along with two young women friends, I was called upon to serve their table. We had been doing this same job for years, and thought we knew how to run things in our "style."

That year, after only a few days of service, we got a message from Lee delivered in no uncertain terms. "Lee wants me to tell you that your service of the meals is 'off,'" the messenger said. "You are acting like a group of teenagers in *la-la* land."

We were shocked! We had never received such feedback before, from Arnaud or from Lee, whom we held with the highest esteem. Devastated, we cried; we talked about what to do; we tried to justify ourselves. How to "fix" whatever was off?

Later during the visit, we were all invited to a special meal held at an elder student's elegant home near the Hauteville ashram. We were told that the hostess would be handling all the service and that we were to enjoy ourselves as guests, which we did. It had been such an exhausting few days and we were all so tired that it was a welcome relief.

As the meal continued, however, we noticed that the plate-removal service and the dessert was delayed for some reason. Again, with no warning, we received a communication from one of Lee's devotees.

[continued]

---

25 The French ashram of Arnaud Desjardins.

"Lee wants to know what are you doing eating?" Obviously, Lee didn't understand.

"We were invited as guests," I answered the messenger, who took our response back to Lee.

But that wasn't the end of it. Within a few minutes the messenger was back with Lee's instruction: "You are *always* serving, and you are *always* at Hauteville." These words were spoken in a normal tone of voice, but we heard them like shouts and they hit us like punches. Shocked. Embarrassed. Offended. We each left the table to find our composure in the bathroom, where we cried bitterly, defending ourselves as best we could from what felt like the most unfair indictment.

Nonetheless, with the last efforts we could muster, we exited to the kitchen where we saw immediately what was needed to carry the meal forth. We served the dessert and handled the situation in as gracious a manner as we could.

At the conclusion of the evening, as Lee and his company were leaving, he stopped in front of us as we gathered at the door to say goodbye. With a soft sincerity he said, "Thank you." His genuine regard was undeniable.

Still Always Serving

By the next day our little team was determined to give up any casualness about our way of working and just dig in. Instead of trying to eat between serving the food courses, we stationed ourselves close to the tables, always watching to see what was needed, ready to take away the empty plates. We were vigilant, fully present. Lee and Arnaud said nothing, but several other devotees, noticing our stance, questioned us: "Why are you standing here?" To which we simply replied, "This is our job." Some, I think, were reassuring us that we could relax a bit. But we continued our new "style," which seemed like a much needed upscale and felt so right!

On his last morning with us at Hauteville, our messenger was back with a final communication from Lee. "He is saying a big thank you to you all."

We politely received the words, but slightly dismissively, knowing that thanks are the normal things that occur at the end of a job. Our messenger detected our dismissive attitude immediately. "No," she said firmly, almost sternly. The power in her words carried Lee's blessing. "This is not about getting a high mark on some test. This is a *real* Thank You." This *was* a *real* thank you.

Visit from a Sheikh

An American Sufi sheikh was in Germany with his students and wanted to visit with Lee and his large traveling party. Lee was on a band tour with Shri at the time and his whole group would be staying for a week at the sangha household near Freiburg. The sheikh told Lee that he would come with three students. Lee called me from the road to check in.

"Can the sangha host them?" he asked.

"Sure, no problem," I answered.

Lee then turned the planning and organizing of the visit with the sheikh over to me. The sangha there would be hosting the sheikh and his students for meals and extensive events for three days.

Three days before they arrived, Lee called me again. He got straight to the point.

"He's coming with thirty-five people, not three," he said.

Pause. I knew what was coming next.

"Can you make that work?" Lee's question contained no pressure to just do it; he was genuinely asking me. He expected me to make a responsible decision on his behalf. Could we handle it? I hesitated for a moment, thinking over the situation. It would be a real challenge for us. I would make the decision, but it was the members of the sangha in Germany who would have to pull off all the work—meals and meeting spaces, clean up, shopping and all that goes with hosting and hospitality, Hohm Community style.

"Yes," I answered. Somehow, we did it all. It was the way Lee trained us over many years, to offer hospitality, to say yes in the moment, to stretch beyond what we think we can do.

That's Why

Lee was speaking at a seminar near Munich, Germany that I had organized for my teacher at the time. I had no experience with this American teacher, but I found him to be attractive. I enjoyed his sense of humor and his arrogance! At the same time, he was kind and friendly with his own students and there was no drama going on around him. This I found very refreshing and interesting. After only a week in his company during the seminar in Munich, I asked him if I could visit him in Arizona. I traveled to the States and spent three months at his ashram. I soon realized that he was the teacher I wanted to work with, and I started organizing teaching events for him in Germany.

When my previous teacher found out about my decision, he was angry. He flatly refused to see me anymore, but the next time he saw Lee, he complained bitterly. Later, one of Lee's students who had witnessed this, told me about their exchange.

"Why do you want him (using my name) for a student? He has a huge ego. His ego is so big, he can't even get through the door!" my old teacher groused.

Lee answered, "That's why I want him."

You Have to Be Dirt!

In February 1994, I was in training to become an ashram cook and had purchased some exotic veggies to replace the baked potatoes that we often had several times a week. When Lee saw what I was doing he was more than annoyed.

"We are in a spiritual community. We don't need to try out new foods. I could eat steamed spinach every day for the rest of my life and I would be fine with it. This thing about trying new things is just about your own boredom."

He was preparing dinner for our weekly gathering at the time, and we were facing each other across one of the kitchen counters. He yelled again: "To be a *tenzo*[27] you have to be dirt! You understand?! Dirt! You have to be nobody!"

A moment later his mood had changed completely, and he was joking with me about all the fun I would have on our upcoming trip to France. "Don't worry," he said, referring to my apparent mistake. His eyes were brimming with humor and delight.

---

[27] *tenzo:* the title given to the cook and person responsible for everything related to food in a Buddhist monastery.

A Longing Dream

A devotee who had never met Lee, but who knew many of his senior students, once reported an exquisite dream. The dreamer recalled a sense of anticipation that ran throughout her whole body as she slept. Then, in a dream, a beautiful man arrived, and immediately she knew it was Lee, although she had only ever seen him in photographs, or read his words in books.

"He touches my arm, lightly" she reported, "and then gently kisses my face." For days afterward she was in a rare state of sweet longing. "It was a glimpse from beyond."

Lost and Found

I had moved away from the ashram to live in another state. While in my new home, I bought new clothes and got a fancier, slicker, "city haircut," which I must have been feeling a little self-conscious about. On my first visit back, I met Lee and his family at the Tucson Gem and Mineral show. They sat down to rest and regroup. I went in search of the bathroom. On my return, I look a few wrong turns which delayed my reunion with the group.

Lee looked at me with concern and asked, "Is everything okay? You were gone a long time."

"Yeah, I am fine," I replied apologetically. "I got lost and I couldn't find you."

He smiled at me tenderly and said, "Oh, don't worry about getting lost. I will always find you." Then he paused and added with a smile, "Even if you've changed your hair."

Airline Food

Lee never ate the food served on airplanes, even when hard pressed to do so. Instead, he carried a few snacks—nuts and dried fruit—from the ashram kitchen. On one of our transatlantic flights, an airline hostess was becoming somewhat insistent, apparently concerned that he was not taking any of the food that was offered onboard.

Many of us travelling with Lee were only too happy to indulge in whatever was offered, but Lee never did. Once, when one of his students finally asked him directly about this, Lee simply stated, "I eat my mind."

Love Affair With Food

Right around Christmas, we were to have a feast for eighty-five people. Lee asked me—the ashram cook—to create a menu for the occasion. I prepared five different menus, and he chose one: goose, pumpkin soup, wild rice, chocolate gateau and more.

There was lots of preparation and planning. Things went well, and Lee was excited. His relationship to the kitchen, to one's cooking, and to food in general, was almost childlike. On this occasion, as on many others, he danced through the kitchen like a child drunk on aromas, delighted with anticipation, enchanted by the last-minute surprises, such as unexpected condiments, chocolate sauces, or sprinkles of nuts.

And . . . he *never* tasted something before a meal. He never compromised his unwavering sense of elegance and impeccability by sticking his fingers into icing or grabbing up premature spoonsful of relishes and sauces. He never checked the taste of anything or corrected my seasoning. He waited until the meal to savor it all.

I found that he was teaching me, with very little input, about refining my cooking. If he enjoyed the dish, then I could safely assume that the recipes worked, the spices were harmonious and so forth. And, he *did* tell me when they obviously did not.

Apples and Bananas

Sometimes Lee got so excited over what he was going to have for lunch. First thing in the morning he planned out what choice piece of fruit he would have. A common choice was a single, green, Granny Smith apple. He'd inspect it and then place it in the drawer of the refrigerator, and God forbid anyone else touched that apple. He might even mention it a couple of times between breakfast and lunch, just like a kid. "I'm starving!" he might say. "Can't wait to bite into that green apple!"

One morning he was contemplating which banana to take on his trip to Phoenix. He looked at the bunch with raised shoulders, clasped hands near his face, and excitedly said, "I haven't had a banana in over a week! I can't wait."

More Than Woman

It was during a 1990 seminar on the ashram celebrating sexuality and power. Lee gave us an exercise to dress as the opposite sex, and he participated with enthusiasm: his curly hair was coiffed back from his face, his fingernails were painted, and he wore a pink sweatshirt saying "Jewish Princess" sensuously draped from one shoulder, with makeup, leg warmers, painted toenails. As we sat on the floor of the dining room, he occasionally rose to get more food. His movements were amazingly smooth, almost more feminine than any woman I knew, but neither fragile nor exaggerated in any way.

While he looked like a woman, he presented himself no differently from how he moved or acted on any other day. Lee seemed neither male nor female to me—or, actually, both.

Food Glorious Food

In 1985, after an exceptionally long stretch of an austere vegetarian diet with little variation, Lee suggested that we drive to Phoenix for a hamburger blowout and a rock concert. The restaurant was absolute cacophony: juke box playing, loudspeakers calling out orders, and the smell of hot oil on the grill and onions being fried. The burgers were half-pound top sirloin, and the place had a forty-foot-long fixings bar. There was kraut and pickles and ten varieties of relish, onions, tomatoes, mushrooms to smother, and every kind of cheese imaginable. There were baskets of fries and onion rings large enough to feed a family of six. For drinks, root beers and shakes of every flavor.

Lee himself concocted a huge burger, and the rest of us followed suit. We "raw food devotees" had a spread to match any gang of teenagers in America.

The next day Lee's observations of the night came in the form of a note: "Oh, if only we could engage sadhana as we engaged the hamburgers and ice cream of yesterday."

No Heroes Needed

A longtime devotee had been in a fairly serious car accident which had required surgery, stitches and a cast on his leg. He lived in Colorado, and rather than missing a Celebration, he took a plane to be here at the ashram. Sunday night, as the darshan continued, the devotee approached the master to offer prasad, hobbling up to the front of the hall with his cane. Several others in attendance were visibly moved by his "heroic" effort. Later, Lee gave a discourse on practice. Describing our patronizing, romanticized and sympathetic attitude toward this devotee, he said, "He only did what any good devotee would do. Nothing heroic! Nothing spectacular. He simply came here to offer prasad."

Experience at Death

One of Lee's German devotees came to live on the ashram for ten months prior to her death. The morning that our sangha friend died, and within half an hour of her passing, Lee came to the room where her body lay.

One of the women devotees who had cared for her over many months read the Death Prayer, a set of "instructions" that Lee had written. The prayer speaks to the newly departed soul, urging her to enter the clear light, the "Source of All." The practice of reading the prayer is to sensitize ourselves to the mood and body of the deceased, and to continue reading until it becomes clear that the prayer has been "heard."

After the reader had completed the prayer twice, Lee himself stood up, took the text and spoke it in a commanding, energetic voice. As I listened, I could almost imagine the her spirit leaping for joy at this familiar and all-powerful sound—that same voice she had studied and contemplated during her years in his company.

When he concluded, he handed the paper back, smiled broadly at the rest of us, and encouraged us to keep reading until we had the sense that she had "moved on." Then he left the room.

Just as he turned to leave, he looked at me and directed me to close the woman's eyes. Her face was tight, so Lee suggested that we keep up the prayer until her eyes relaxed and closed a bit. Nearly an hour later there was a marked difference in her face, and the eyes relaxed slightly. At that point we stopped the prayer (all agreed that something had changed!) and began to prepare her body for burial.

Crazy Movies

Lee loved to go to movies. Once, before his anticipated visit to Boulder, Colorado, we all considered which movies we might suggest seeing with him during this visit, and finally settled on a few, including a popular new release that was said to be artistic and significant.

When Lee arrived and heard our plan, he rolled his eyes and moaned a bit at our choices. But when someone announced that "Naked Gun 33 1/3—the Final Insult" was in town, he perked up, and off we went. This would have been the last film we would have suggested, as it was full of crude humor.

After the movie credits had rolled, Lee commented with satisfaction: "Now that's *my* kind of movie!"

It's About Time

In 1999 or 2000, I had travelled from Canada to the Prescott ashram as a guest for a Celebration event. While I had never met Lee, I had read a few of his books and knew of him through others. The night I arrived, late in the evening, I was shown to my room, and given directions for how to find the Tavern—the late-night gathering place I had heard of, where Lee met with students over tea and quiet conversation.

As I navigated the narrow and dark staircase to the Tavern, which was on the second floor of the main building, I felt an extreme sense of discomfort bordering on anxiety. Actually, I felt ready to bolt. This was all so new, and just too strange, I remember thinking. I fantasized grabbing my backpack from my room and heading for the road where I would hitchhike to the airport and get back to my own life.

When I got to the head of the stairs, however, and stood before the curtain at the entrance to the Tavern, I dredged up all the courage I could muster, took a deep breath and entered the room. I had been instructed in the protocol of the space, so I stepped in, joined my hands in the *anjali* mudra,[28] closed my eyes and bowed in the direction in which Lee was seated.

As I raised my head and opened my eyes, Lee was *right there*, catching my gaze with intensity. Although no words were exchanged, I immediately felt a communication through his eyes, that said: "Well, you finally got here. It took you long enough!" With that, I relaxed completely, and even began to laugh, quietly, interiorly. He too seemed to be laughing.

---

28 A yogic hand gesture, placing the palms together, fingers extended upward, at the center of the chest. An acknowledgement of respect.

Dancing Krishna

During a darshan in September 1982, amidst enthusiastic chanting of *Hare Krishna*—which Lee particularly liked—he abruptly stood up from his seat at the front of the room and began to dance in a most childlike and ecstatic fashion. The room went wild. Suddenly, everyone was on their feet. Many of the women were jumping and running about, their arms ecstatically raised towards the heavens. The last word I had written in my notebook that night was "abandonment." I too then found myself dancing and shouting with joy. Some of the other men also danced, some simply stood up and watched, some gently swayed to the music. The din was so loud that the chant could barely be heard. Lee, having danced briefly, again sat in his chair and watched the Celebration with delight.

As the chanting wound down, he smiled broadly. "Was that for real or did I just imagine it?" he said. Laughter followed. "That's a bit of what I was talking about last week at the public talk in Boulder," he added. During that visit he had said that his dharmic discourse was secondary to the communication that could be made, and received, during a session of chanting. It was true—no words could have moved us in the way the chanting and dancing had done.

Our Big Surprise

After the first Tavern had been held initiated on the Prescott ashram, I returned to the Boulder household where my husband and I were living. Enthusiastically, we created our own version of a Tavern and planned a special initiatory gathering for a few days later.

One day before the scheduled event, I got a phone call from Arizona. It was Lee. "Don't tell anyone," he began, "but I'm coming to town and I want you to pick me up at the airport tomorrow. And, don't tell anyone that I'm coming."

This was incredible! Unbelievable! How did he know this? I couldn't remember any conversation in which he'd been informed of our planned evening.

Now, I had to keep his visit a secret for over twenty-four hours, even from my husband. What sort of excuse could I use that would get me out of the house to make the two-hour roundtrip to the Denver airport and then arrive back just in time?

Two hours before Lee's expected arrival, having arranged for almost everything, I excused myself from my kitchen duties saying that I needed to go to the store for more special ingredients for the meal preparation. My heart was racing and took a leap when I saw him walk into the waiting area alone. It had never occurred to me that he would have no other sangha or family with him.

"I didn't mean that you had to pick me up *yourself*," he blurted out.

"You said not to tell anyone, and I would have had to tell someone else if I didn't come alone."

[continued]

Immediately, his face brightened into a radiant grin, "Great!" he said, obviously pleased.

On the trip back to Boulder I entered a completely timeless space, and finally relaxed into the circumstance of just being with him. We realized we would get back early, so he suggested we stop for a Coke at Denny's.

When at last we pulled up to the house in Boulder, I was beside myself with excitement. "I'll wait in the car," he said. "Come and notify me when everybody is in place inside." I agreed.

As I entered the house empty-handed, and with just enough time to change," my husband rushed over to me. "What have you been doing?" I don't remember what silly excuse I made as I hurried upstairs to get ready.

"I'll join you and the others in the Tavern in a few minutes," I called back.

The other sangha arrived one by one over the next few minutes, all in a celebratory mood of sharing communion in this new space. After a short time I silently got up as if to attend to some serving details, walked outside and informed Lee that everyone had arrived. He had changed his clothes in the car, and I led him through the dark up to the house and then to the door of the Tavern.

Without a word he entered, bowed slightly and took the seat that we had kept in honor of him, which otherwise would have remained empty tonight. One by one the guests looked up to greet the new arrival. Each one beheld our beloved guru. No apparition! The room filled with sweet gasps, laughter and cries of delight as we settled into that long intimate night of sheer awe in his company and the company of one another. Lee was absolutely radiant.

He Writes

At a Celebration in 1994, one of the senior devotees explained that she was collecting stories of Lee for a book. [The one you have in your hands now, thirty years later!] She handed out small yellow pads of paper and asked that anyone who took one must promise to fill it with stories.

I took one, as I have many stories, and like to write. Many others took them too. I noted with a smile that Lee himself enthusiastically took one and immediately started to write in it.

Special Medicine?

In the last years of his life, despite his ongoing struggles with a painful throat,[29] Lee continued to perform with his bands. It was one of his great pleasures, and his great work, or so we understood.

One night he asked my help before a gig. Did I have anything thing that would relieve his pain and allow him to sing as he wished?

I did have something, really strong, which I knew would numb his throat. The pain would be relieved, temporarily, I told him, but if he wanted long term results, he should not sing full out. . .overstressing his voice.

The next day he came to me to express his gratitude for my remedy. I had already heard from other sangha mates that Lee had sung with abandon that night! Exactly what I had asked him to avoid. But. . .

"Your help really worked," he said, rather apologetically, but sincerely. He was not going to stop, no matter what!

---

[29] In 2010, Lee died from cancer of the throat and tongue.

The Shakti on the Bus

I was sitting in a café with Lee when I began to have "crazy kriyas"—manifestations of shakti energy involuntarily shooting through my body, causing my arms to vibrate and my body to shake. This type of phenomena often happened to me, and to some others when in Lee's energy field. Observing me, Lee said: "I saw a woman on a bus the other day doing just that."

Me (in my usual self-deprecating and satirical way): "Yes, she was psychotic, wasn't she?"

Lee: "I don't know. Maybe she had a guru. You never can tell."

The Famous Flamenco Dance

I was raised in a "what will people think" household. I am so often concerned with how others would look at what I did that my actions are hampered. This was especially difficult in terms of acting spontaneously. Lee had frequently pointed out that, in any situation more people have never seen me before and will probably never see me again, so why should I worry about what they think?

He has demonstrated this in many ways, but the all-time standout time occurred in a crowded movie theatre lobby as we were waiting to go into a show. Someone jostled my elbow, and I spilled my popcorn onto the floor. Lee immediately began doing a Flamenco dance, in the spirit of Jose Greco, on top of the spilled popcorn. Needless to say, the crowd gave us as much space as possible, and by the time he finished his dance, the spilled popcorn was reduced to a little more than white specs. Through my embarrassment, I saw the humor in his actions. What's more, the world had not come to an end. We went into the show, Lee acting as if nothing out the ordinary had happened . . . while one of our group, at a nod from Lee, stayed outside for a while to clean things up.

Diamonds in the Rough

Lee had agreed to allow me to move to the ashram, despite my obvious emotional insecurity at the time. In his great kindness, he had asked the sangha to support me however they could. One evening, after I had been away at a family wedding, I returned to the ashram where I met up with Lee and a small group of the sangha in the evening tea space.

Despite his usual gentleness with me, on this night he was fairly shouting questions and observations in a long and vital interchange, focused around the way I was dealing (like an immature child) with my family of origin.

Sometime following this evening encounter, Lee commented to the whole group as we gathered for an after-dinner talk, saying: "You are all diamonds in various stages of having 'matrix' removed and being 'cut.' I already know what kind of diamond most of you are. What color, if there are flaws, how you should be cut and so on. In D's case [I was D.], the diamond I know is there has been obscured from view by matrix. We have begun to uncover it, and that to me is exciting."

Small Kindness, Small Miracle

At darshan, I kept wanting to go in and give Lee my prasad, but each time I tried, my baby started to yell. Several people offered to hold him, but the child wasn't having any of it. I finally decided to give it one last try. After that, I would give up if it didn't work. I took my child in my arms as I went forward and gave Lee my prasad. He gave me back a piece of toffee, which I unwrapped and automatically gave to my son. Then, I went and sat down. Lee then threw a second toffee my way. It sailed down the center aisle, and descended two meters in front of me, bounced off someone's foot and finally landed straight in my lap. The message was very clear. "You don't have to give absolutely *everything* away to your child. This one is for you!" Within a couple of minutes my child was asleep and I could join in the chanting.

Translating for Him

The first time I translated for Lee I asked him to go slowly, meaning not to speak too many sentences at one go, because my concentration and memory are not very good. He carefully obliged.

In the process, however, I was frequently distracted, and would occasionally look at my watch when it seemed like the talk was going on for such a long time. As soon as I lost attention, I would feel panic arising, as I knew I had missed several pieces of what he was saying. Then, I would have to ask him, "What was the last thing you said?"

"Sure," he would say, and then repeat himself more slowly, always gracious in his response, no matter how many times this happened, and even when the audience was not so patient.

First Time, He or She?

I was traveling with my ex-wife through the Southwest to meet some old friends. I had been in another spiritual school for fifteen years and considered myself quite adept at practice and intuition about the work. My ex-wife asked if we could stop at an ashram in Prescott, as her mother had received help from the guru there when she was going through a hard time, and I agreed.

We finally arrived at the ashram an hour late and the meal we had been expected to attend was already over. Apparently, people had been waiting for us with more anticipation than I had for such a meeting. As we stood in the dining room speaking with a number of people, while a dog was running around barking as someone tried to coax it outside. A hippie-looking guy came to the door and made a few announcements. He obviously held some authority, so I assumed he was probably a manager around the place.

No one had actually introduced us to Lee yet, and as I overheard my ex-wife talking to someone about "she" this and "she" that, I wondered if perhaps Lee might actually be a woman. I wracked my brain trying to recall if previously Lee had been referred to as "he." I decided that, since I was such an intuitive practitioner, I could just relax and assume that I would know who Lee was as soon as I set eyes on "him/her/it."

The hippie-guy began showing us around the ashram, chatting about this and that, and even asking me about the nature of my previous spiritual work. Surely this couldn't be Lee, I reasoned. Lee would certainly know about all such things.

Meanwhile, I scanned the area holding out for the possibility that some statuesque blond would glide up and reveal herself to be the "real" Lee.

Following the tour, we were invited to join in a spontaneous "darshan," which I understood was some sort of get together held a few times per week. Guided to the main house, we entered a living room of sorts with one easy chair and a bowl of candy at the front. To my amazement, our tour guide took the front chair and began tossing candy to the assembled crowd. *Shit*! This was the anticlimax to the whole game for me. By the time this gathering thing was over I was more than ready to get back on the road.

When we got to Sedona and met up with our friends there, I regaled them with the story of this weird assembly and my confusion about the "he" or "she" of things. Back home after several weeks, I heard from my mother-in-law that Lee had informed her of our visit and noted that I seemed to be a sincere and honest person, but obviously "he doesn't know anything about spiritual life."

It still amazes me that after such a start I would find myself at his feet, a devotee, living within close proximity with him and this community for years.[30]

---

30 This devotee eventually died on the ashram, having served the sangha for many years.

Down in the Dirt

When I first came to the school, I attributed superhuman strength to the guru, along with overlays of father, friend, savior etc. Witnessing Lee's ordinary vulnerability to life, his own and ours, was sometimes unsettling to these projections. I had to work to somehow see my teacher through and in these veils.

A striking example of his willingness to sacrifice these powerful images was his participation with us in a psychological process called "The Game." Lee had invited the facilitator of this process to visit our ashram, because he respected the man who designed it, acknowledged its effectiveness, and wanted us to have the advantage of some strong confrontation with our psychological knots. The Game was designed to do exactly that.

Following his lead, most of us signed up for it, and some devotees came from out of town to participate. What no one knew in advance was that Lee himself would sit in the circle with us. Not as an observer, but as a full player in a process that would deeply prod one's personal history and reveal more than one might expect. What amazed me throughout was Lee's unabashed vulnerability, remorse over his own shortcomings, and deep resonance with the pain and suffering of others. He was down in the dirt with us and, at the same time, not caught in the twisted machinations of ego that most of us expertly devise as strategies for survival. He was simply alive, present and receptive to whatever was said by any of us or said about or to him.

I also saw Lee shed tears, sometimes in the midst of an anguishing encounter within the group, and at other times, simple tears of obvious joy.

Embarrass Me

During one Celebration Lee gave us the exercise to embarrass him, while giving no hints as to why, or what he would consider embarrassing. As the days went by the devotees tried all sorts of pranks, including one of his household members who gave him a big kiss, in public. This drew lots of laughter but didn't embarrass him, he said.

As the master emerged from the darshan hall one afternoon, one of the long-time male devotees stopped him in the corridor and began rather dramatically to perform a ritual foot washing (*pada pooja*).

At the final darshan of the weekend, Lee said that no one had fully succeeded in the task, but that this male devotee's act had come closest. "A gesture of *real* devotion," he said, "would truly embarrass him."

Never Lose Sight

In Germany in 1990, while touring Europe with my new community friends, I was videotaping the band gigs and being in Lee's company daily. At this point, I did not consider myself his student or devotee. I was simply along for the ride!

Late one afternoon, in the seminar house, I was walking up the steps to the third-floor landing where a large picture window gave me a view of the whole backyard. From this view I could see him clearly, sitting on a bench, with children playing on the lush green lawn around him. He sat with such an unhurried mood. He had no plans, no nothing. He was simply waiting.

I was transfixed here, and somehow I couldn't leave to continue up to the next floor which was my destination. The soft breeze of the afternoon floated around him, obviously caressing his skin. "I am in love," was all I knew.

As I stood still and watched, other people came by, stopped, talked with him for a moment or two, and then moved on. I could not walk away. Tears were streaming down my face. "Who is he?" "Can I go to him?" "Should I?" Other people passed me quietly on the stairs.

I sensed that he didn't care what I knew about the teaching, the dharma, the school, the "meaning" of a spiritual master, or whatever. Yet, I sensed—I *can* be with him...but should I actually *ask* him?

No, no...my mind argued. "You don't need to ask him anything. Just never lose sight of him! *Never* lose sight of him."

After a time he left the bench and walked barefoot across the lawn and into the house below me.

Impossible Task

Visiting the ashram and spending time with Lee, one day he mentioned that I might be interested in writing a book. By this time in our relationship, after many years of study with him and many years of missing opportunities for real growth, I immediately said, “Yes!”

A moment later, however, the “mind” started to list the million reasons why such a task was impossible. But it was too late. I had committed.

I started figuring that, with all my other work and responsibilities, I could maybe cobble together such a book within the next three to four years. It was doable. So, I asked Lee, “How long would I have to complete this project, Sir?”

Lee immediately turned to the Hohm Press publisher, asking when a manuscript would be needed for next year’s release. “Around the first of August . . . this year,” the publisher reported. This encounter with Lee took place on June first. The mind was horrified. “Make it about 100 pages or so,” Lee said, supplying me with details. “And it should be such that a novice reading it would get immediate help, simple and clear; the same for a very advanced, senior student.”

When I got home from the trip, I sat down at the typewriter and prayed for help. Very quickly the entire table of contents revealed itself to me, and every step of the way I received the same unmistakable help and inspiration. Miraculously, in the first week of August the manuscript was done.

The Prayer Beads

In late 1989 I was going on a trip to the east coast. The night before I was to leave, Lee came by my room and handed me a set of mala beads,[31] simply saying, "Here, wear these." How did he know that I had wanted to ask him for weeks now if I could buy some mala beads from him but had not gotten around to it? How did he know that for days before I had been in great turmoil, feeling very lost, crying out in my prayers for help, not even sure what help I was needing? And now, just when I needed some encouragement before going away, and just when I had given up on asking for beads, he arrived, placing this beautiful set of beads into my hands. I am still in awe.

31 Traditional prayer beads (like a rosary) used to count one's mantras. The Hindu mala contains 108 beads. They are made of many different substances, from gems and stones to seeds or even beads fashioned from rose petals.

Prasad for Years

My job on the ashram was to answer phones from early morning until breakfast, which meant that I never attended the community meditation space for thirteen years, but meditated in the office, sitting on an office chair, alert to the phone.

Every morning that he was in residence for those thirteen years, Lee came down to the office immediately after morning practice and placed a piece of candy prasad into my hands. While those in the meditation hall would receive their prasad from the pujari of the day, mine was always directly from his hands. On a few rare instances when he was unable to meet me there, he had one of his children come down and deliver the gift to me. "From Baba,"[32] the child would announce, as she placed the gift in my waiting hand.

[32] Baba ("father, grandfather, wise old man, sir") is an honorific term, used as a mark of respect to refer to Hindu ascetics (sannyasis) and Sikh gurus, or as a suffix or prefix to their names.

The Worry Stone

One evening, after Lee's return from a trip to Mexico, he carried into the Darshan Hall a plastic bag filled with small stones he had acquired on the beaches he visited. I had to leave the room for a short time, and when I returned, he had apparently given a stone to each student present, choosing the stones with care, as though someone's name were written on each one. When I came into the hall, he tossed me a stone and said that mine was a "worry stone" and that it could be held or fingered when one was troubled.

I was grateful to receive any gift from him, but I didn't really grasp the significance of a worry stone, and he didn't seem interested in elucidating on the use of them. Later that night, I placed the stone on the small table near my bed, and though I looked at the stone on occasion, I didn't feel moved to use it in any way.

A few weeks later, a child was born on the ashram. It had been a very exciting day for all of us and the grounds were charged with a highly energized atmosphere. Toward the end of the day, the energy I had been feeling began to manifest as a bad headache. I went to darshan, and afterwards fell into bed. On impulse I picked up the worry stone and placed it on my forehead. It felt cool against the hot pain of the headache. Immediately, I felt the energy in my head begin to move, much like an inverted whirlpool, into the stone. The area of skin under that stone got extremely hot and gradually the pain became less intense. Finally, I removed the stone and quickly fell into a deep sleep. The next morning, I woke without a trace of a headache, and in fact felt wonderfully refreshed. I held the stone in amazement and had an odd sensation that the stone's purpose was to serve me when I was in need.

Later, I was surprised and moved to learn from a friend precisely how Lee had chosen *my* worry stone. Having fingered through them, he chose a particular stone and said, "Ah, here's a heavy one." Knowing my tendency to "heavy worry," he looked around the room for me and asked, "Where's T.? This one is perfect for her."

Happy About the Music

For months, Lee's attention had been on his work with the band. At one after-dinner talk he had asked for questions, and then quietly and patiently addressed them, one by one.[33] After an hour of some rather lackluster exchanges, someone asked him something about the band and his music. Immediately his face brightened, he sat up higher in his chair, and his words poured out without hesitation. The whole room also became lighter, brighter. It was literally as if someone had turned on the lights, realizing that dusk had settled in the space.

33 After-dinner talks were given by Lee every Tuesday or Thursday evening for decades. Lee would comment on books he was studying, or give spontaneous teachings, or speak to the practical matters of life in the community.

"Relax, Will Ya"

LGB (*liars, gods and beggars*) was performing in the back room at the Warehouse, a Prescott venue, during a Celebration gig. I was very nervous about playing and being a bit dramatic about it, pacing and clearing my throat and fidgeting. Just as we stepped up to the stage, Lee turned to me and said, in a pleading tone of voice, "Would you *please* stop it. You're making *me* nervous."

What Audience Is That?

In the early days of LGB we would meet five minutes before going onstage. "The Huddle" we called it. Sometimes we gathered in silence, sometimes simply to release our nervousness. Once in Germany, he spoke to us about how we were not there to play to the audience in the club. He said, "The audience we play to is always the same, wherever we go. No matter when we play, *that* audience is the one we should be playing to."

Shortly after that, back in the States, we played a gig in Phoenix, with only a few people present. At that point, we *got* what Lee was talking about. We played to that "other audience" and even with only two or three people in the bar, we played full out, as if we were standing in front of three hundred.

The Shape Shifter

It had been obvious to me for many years that Lee was a "shape shifter." I've seen him in darshan take on any number of personae, but it became most spectacular during his performances with LGB. By nature, at least by my observation, Lee was very quiet and even introverted (he said the same about himself). I would describe him as sort of a Clark Kent, the "mild-mannered reporter," character. When he stepped onto the stage, however, he passed through an invisible phone booth and emerged as Superman and Mick Jagger all rolled into one as he strutted, gyrated and became arrogant, angry or beguiling, or whatever manifestation the song, crowd or energy called forth.

When he sang "Little Red Rooster" he usually sat in a chair rocking it back and forth as if it were an old rocking chair. He actually "became" an old, grey-haired Black blues-singer sitting on a front porch somewhere down South. In a song called "Sugar Shock" where he sang about obsession and "eating myself to death," he seemed to gain weight right before our eyes. At times, it seemed he could almost burst, he got so big! In his song "Spite" his eyes showered the audience with sparks, making you want to hide from the anger he was apparently spewing out. In "Front Door Man" there was so much sex and energy about him that I honestly got turned on. When he concluded with "Ordinary Man," he flipped back and forth between being self-assured and more than capable into a simple guy just wanting to be himself again.

At the end of each set, Lee stepped back "through the phone booth" and once more became the quiet Clark Kent.

[continued]

The transformation was so complete that he actually became "invisible."

At a gig on the band tour of the South, in Little Rock, Arkansas, a blues-harp musician in another band watched Lee carefully throughout his performances and enthusiastically applauded him at the end of his solo. Less than half an hour later, as Lee walked to the back of the room to buy a t-shirt, that same musician was behind the concession table. Looking directly at Lee, he asked, "Are you with the LGB band? They are really good."

How could this man not have recognized that Lee was the star of that show? He didn't even make the connection. Lee was just an ordinary guy, back through the phone booth, invisible once again.

Lullaby Meditations

In the early years in New Jersey, when many of us were just learning about meditation, Lee would guide us in the process.

I remember vividly that he asked us to close our eyes and get comfortable, which we did. Many people were stretched out every which way, all over the place, in all kinds of positions. He spoke the guided meditation to us softly, as if he were talking to a child, calling upon us to trust and embrace the presence of God wherever we went, and to always know that we were not alone. He asked us to remember his love and support for us, and to know that in times of crisis and great need he would always be right here with us whenever we called, now and forever.

I felt cradled in his hands during these moments, like I was being blessed and joyously carried by the God I had never really known. His words were actually more like a lullaby. Those meditations were rare but so precious and were usually filled with far more silence than words. He often asked us to "love one another" and to enjoy and appreciate the very things right in front of our eyes.

Making Plans

I was sweating the details of preparing for some trip I was taking and helping organize for the sangha. Lee shook his head at my list of questions, saying, "There's no need to make plans until there is a need to make plans." I use that statement with myself and others many times. It helps a lot!

A Crazy Question

During darshan I was just about to ask Lee for his assessment of the fact that this spiritual school of ours is still so small. But then, as I listened, he made the reason eminently clear, saying that if he put himself in a monastery or on a mountaintop somewhere, and set up really strict rules and laws with lots of traditional trappings, he would probably get a very large following, in view of the American insanity relative to spiritual life. Instead of that, he picks up the mail, answers the office phone, and lives a rather ordinary life. Few people know that Prescott, Arizona is the site of the most radical spiritual school in America.

Flying Answer

We had all been studying the books by Carlos Castaneda religiously, and Lee often talked about this material, quoting from the books in his darshan. One evening, along with my offering of prasad, I handed him a slip of paper that contained a question pertaining to this material. Then, I returned to my seat in the back row. During the chanting, Lee wrote something in his notepad, tore out the page, then proceeded to fold the paper several times. Next thing I knew, he was poised with his right arm cocked and throwing a paper airplane all the way across the room. It soared cleanly over everyone's heads and landed squarely in my lap. I unfolded it, and there was the answer to my question.

In Hard Times

Decades ago, sometime in 1977, Lee had asked a devotee to do a special research project and to report her findings to the group. What she shared was electrifying, for that time, and more so as I recall it today in 2022.

She talked to us about cataclysmic upheavals in the Earth's climate and geography; about the Edgar Casey readings; and about frozen mammoths discovered perfectly intact in the Siberian tundra. She presented a literal onslaught of historical, archaeological, and geographic documentation of not one but indeed several accounts of repeated worldwide disasters and the unexplained extinction of species both in prehistoric and in human history as well.

When she had finished her report and enough of us were sufficiently stunned, it was clear that an impression had indeed been made. Lee then spent the rest of the evening stressing the *absolute importance of community and mutual wholehearted support* for one another as being literally the only way to survive hard times. He encouraged us to stick with him at all costs since he himself planned to be "somewhere else" when disaster hit.

We were all amazed at the way the whole evening evolved, and our faces must have shown this. Looking around, Lee simply smiled and said, "Don't worry. It's not time to go *just yet.* Just be ready to drop everything and leave, when it is."

He Opens the Door

One day in late 1989, I was feeling upset with Lee for something he had said to me. My emotions were all over the place—anger, fear, pain. I was just about to leave the house carrying a laundry basket out to the clothesline when I heard someone open a door nearby. I prayed that it wasn't Lee, as I was too much in recoil to want to interact with him. But a moment later he was there, holding the door open for me, gently. I would have to pass within inches of him now. So, I kept my head down, making my closed-off condition even more obvious. "Thank you," I said, somewhat coldly.

Softly, he replied, "You can still be angry and look at me." I froze for a moment because I really didn't think I could give up my contraction that easily. Still, that simple gesture of opening the door for me had touched my heart. It broke a little.

He Waits for Me

The spiritual master always knew when I was surrendered to him, when I was being "that which nothing can take root in."[34] He knew when I had found the living teaching in my body, and he would always let me know in some subtle or direct way that he knew what was occurring in my inner world. Even if there were years in between these experiences, even when I was (in my view) on the "outs" with him, as soon as I "found" him again within myself, he would let me know that he was always just waiting for me to find him again. Nothing more. His *only* desire was that I reconnect to him.

Lee supported all my worldly endeavors—business travel, work with other students—but these were never his greatest wish for me. He only ever wanted me to be at one with him.

In 1978, at a time when I was feeling alienated and at odds with Lee on many issues, I attended a conference in Atlanta and spent an evening with another man who was an avid student of the Work. We talked endlessly about the Path and our practice, and about our teachers. This conversation opened me so wide that my resistances dissolved, and I felt Lee's presence for days and days.

Arriving back in New Jersey, I walked in the door of my apartment just as the phone rang. It was Lee. He was up at his home about sixty miles away, and he invited me to come right up. At that point, a phone call directly from Lee was a rare occurrence. But, there it was.

He always knew when I "found" him.

---

[34] One of Lee's basic teachings having to do with non-identification.

Changing the Date

In late November 1989 I called the ashram to find out if the date had yet been determined for the next Guru Purnima Celebration (the following July 1990). This was important for me to know since I had been offered a potentially lucrative speaking engagement in July. Still, I didn't want to miss the Celebration.

A senior devotee of Lee's answered the phone and when she heard my question, she asked me to hold while she asked Lee if he had set the date yet for that event. A minute later she was back on the phone. "Wait till you hear what your spiritual master did," she said admiringly. "He said that since your engagement was scheduled for the 13th, the Celebration would begin on the 15th to give you the opportunity to attend."

I hung up the phone in a state of utter amazement. Also, I was laughing with delight, like a child. "Imagine," I reflected, "this is the way that important decisions get made around here!"

He Came to Me

As a new student, and one who had visited the ashram only a few times, I was shy and reticent to join Lee at the evening bridge game at his kitchen table. One night shortly after I arrived, I waited in the hallway near the kitchen while he played, talking with a few of my new acquaintances, stealing a glance or two at him, and also basically "hiding out," even if it was as close to him as I dared to get.

Imagine my shock and surprise when I caught his eye and he immediately got up from the bridge game and stepped out into the hallway to seek me out. "Welcome," he said, so warmly, as he embraced me. His kindness in coming out to find me, when I was too shy to approach him, is a memory I always cherish.

Hearing Voices

Many years ago, when the community was still in New Jersey and Lee ran the bookstore, I was laid up in bed for four months in a back brace, unable to leave the house. I had not seen or spoken to Lee for many weeks, although I always felt his love and support. One day, however, when the pain was especially intense, I was at my wit's end. With a burst of tears, I called Lee up just to say hello. I felt foolish and embarrassed, not knowing what to say, because I actually had nothing to say. I just missed him! It was crazy, knowing how busy he usually was, but my heart cried out anyway and I had to let him know how good it felt just to hear his voice. I told him this, apologetic for bothering him.

"Oh, no," he answered cheerfully. "It's not crazy at all. In fact, I'm glad you called. It's good to hear your voice too."

A long pause followed, but it felt full of deep connection. After almost two minutes of this silence, I was speechless and trembling. "I don't seem to have anything to say," I blurted out again, unable to hold back the tears this time.

"That's okay," he answered. "You don't have to say anything. Let's just stay on the line for a while and hang out together." And we did. Except for the pounding of my heart and an occasional sniffle on my part to check back the tears, we spent five solid minutes in silence, "conversing" without words. It ended when I heard the chimes to his front door jingle and Lee said, "I have to go now. There's someone in the bookstore. Talk to you later."

I went back to bed and was amazed to discover that I was drenched in sweat. A great relief had come over me and I slept peacefully for hours.

A week later, the phone rang in the middle of the afternoon, and when I waddled into the hall to answer it (as I was still wearing my back brace), I was astounded to hear Lee's voice. "Hi, this is me again," he said. "I just called to complete our conversation from the other day." And for the next ten minutes we just hung out on the phone in total silence, exactly as before.

At some point our "conversation" felt complete and we thanked one another and said good-bye. I then hung up the phone, leaned against the wall, and cried.

Seva Master[35]

During the November 1990 Appearance Day (Lee's Birthday) Celebration, as I was staffing the book-display table in the office, I had the chance to observe all the comings and goings in front of the building. I watched Lee at work with two of the men who were cleaning the large BBQ grills that had been used the night before. The grills were coated with soot and grease, making them definitely a nightmare to clean, in my opinion. Yet, the job seemed to actually delight him, and he appeared enthusiastic in his approach to it.

For me this would have been the *most* disagreeable job anyone would be requested to do that weekend, and here was Lee himself doing it, and even seeming to enjoy it.

---

35 *Seva*, or *guru seva*, is service done for the guru or teacher, or for others, with the purest motivation possible.

Nail Polish Lila

As I prepared to visit the Arizona ashram for my first Celebration, I became obsessed with what to wear, how to style my hair and what kind of nail polish would be appropriate…or whether that was even allowed there. (Would I be Revlon-persona-non-grata?)

Normally, these issues are not that major for me. But, as I prepared to take a deeper dive into Lee's world, they suddenly seemed significant.

When I got off the plane and made my way to the ashram, I arrived just in time for Lee's talk. I don't know how to express my enormous relief, and humor, when I walked into the room and saw Lee's hands. His fingernails were perfectly painted with bright red nail polish.

Generosity in Action

As a longtime student of Lee's, I had arrived for a short visit and was asked to help him in the kitchen as he and another cook prepared the evening meal for the sangha. Thrilled at the request for assistance, I was delighted to find him listening to music as he chopped vegetables, and I promptly offered a comment that I too loved this music of Leonard Cohen. Lee was quick to reply, "Oh, that's not Leonard, that's Joe Cocker." Not wanting to contradict him, I simply said, "Oh, um."

The other cook, however, was less reticent to correct Lee's "mistake." "Yes, It's Leonard all right," she interjected, confirming my opinion.

Now, it was Lee's turn to say, "Oh, um," without so much as a word of defense or explanation.

A moment later, he was dancing in place, chopping and dancing and humming the tune. I too was fully delighted, finding him with such joy, spontaneity and energy.

Subtle Teaching Style

Lee's teaching style is often so subtle. He gently told me that a piece of writing I had edited from one of his German students lacked life and he had no inclination to publish it.

I immediately attempted to defend myself, apparently agreeing with him. "Well, yes, I thought so too," I said knowingly. "I was just trying to…" He didn't wait for me to finish, but simply smiled, said nothing, and walked on.

Nothing else needed to be said.

Visionary

During the late 80s and early 90s, Lee made it clear that his rock band—LGB (*liars, gods, and beggars*)—was an essential element of his work with the community. He called the members of any such group a "configuration" and implied that they were chosen for reasons that might not seem obvious but held transformational potential for the members involved. So it was that the six members of LGB included only two who were accomplished musicians. Two others were just barely okay on their instruments, while two were complete beginners. This seemed to me, one of the "barely okays," to be a strange way to plan for the high-level commercial success that Lee declared as his aim. It was an impossible vision, considering who we were. But he firmly held to this intention, no matter what!

Despite our doubts and insecurities, LGB toured the U.S. and Europe, performed on some great stages in summer festivals, and produced seven albums of original music, lyrics by Lee and composition by our own band members. And add to this the enormous energy of a wide range of the sangha who participated at every step of the way!

Amazed

Lee was undoubtedly the driving force behind LGB. His vision was magnetic, and we in the band were only too delighted to follow his lead. Well, particularly at first.

As time went on, however, some of us began to object to his suggestions—like about who should stay in, or who should be out of the band, or how a song should be rendered, or whether a recording was "good enough" or not.

Whatever the objection from one or more of us, Lee just didn't argue. He never power-tripped us. Most often he deferred to us. I was amazed by his surrender and how much he had placed in our hands but, to this day, feel a bit remorseful at how many opportunities I may have missed by holding onto my conventional standards.

Wonder

The desert shimmered with heat as we drove toward the ashram that July (1988). I'd been looking forward to meeting Lee for six months. The last year had brought death and chaos into my life; at last, after years of traveling my own spiritual path, I had the sense that I'd come as far as I could alone. Yet, I had no particular expectation about meeting this teacher. Just an openness tinged with excitement and a small steady flame of longing.

As it was a Sunday, Lee would be giving his formal darshan, which my friend had explained as carefully as she could. Still, I marveled at the moment when, poised at the doorway to the Darshan Hall, my eyes fell on the man who sat silent and still on a dais at one end of a room full of people, movement and sound. Instantaneously, his eagle eyes pierced mine with a ruthless look. Then I was inside and seated, washed in the full sensory impact of the scene—the chanting, the candles and incense, the bright heat of a few dozen devotees crammed into a rather small space. I was fascinated, amazed, and somewhat skeptical. At the same time, I was aware of something deeply familiar in the chanting and the mood.

I had brought fresh raspberries for prasad, and finally, I walked down the aisle to offer my gift. Still standing, I bowed then looked into his eyes with open curiosity. The ruthlessness was gone, and in that moment I fell into the original innocence of my own heart. A spontaneous smile spread across my face at the pure and free feeling of recognition that washed over me. I walked away in wonder—who was this man?

Prayer and Ice Cream

In the early days of the 1970s, when I was brand new to the spiritual scene, I would gather with the group for chanting, sometimes followed by meditation. At the program's end there would always be a period of silence. Then, to close the night, Lee would *pranam* (either to us, or to God, I was never sure which), and he would remain motionless in that posture for a long moment. He was still seated on the floor, cross-legged, and would bend from the waist, placing his forehead to the ground, with his hands stretched out fully in front of him.

The rest of the group would just sit there in the silence, in varying degrees of embarrassment, not knowing what was going on. (I know I surely didn't. I never saw anybody do that kind of thing before.) It felt like prayer.

After that, most of the people would leave almost immediately, in a kind of slow-motion procession towards the door. Then, with Lee in the lead, we all just piled into our cars and vans and headed for the local diner for hamburgers and ice cream.

The Shirt Off My Back

One day Lee walked into the Prescott ashram office where one of the teenagers greeted him and said, “I like that shirt you’re wearing, Lee.”

“Thanks” he replied, “If you want it, you can have it.” Then, in a Humphrey-Bogart-like voice, he added, “I’ll give you the shirt off my back, kid.”

Everyone in the office laughed, enjoying the master’s play. Delightedly, Lee peeled off the shirt and tossed it to the teenager who had complemented him. Then, adding, “It’s good that it’s warm in the office,” as he settled back, shirtless, to his desk to thumb through a magazine.

Nothing Special

When Lee was visiting our home in France, I prepared a glass of grapefruit juice for him since I knew he liked it. Nothing special. But, when I presented it to him after the meal his gratitude was so immense, although he said only a few words. I was drowned in the unfathomable depth of his thanks.

The Giveaway Box

We had a free-exchange box, which we called the Giveaway Box, on the ashram. Friends and guests, or other sangha members, would contribute clothing and other items to this box for the free use of anyone else in the sangha. As I was petite, I could hardly ever find anything in my size. When winter set in, however, I kept checking the box. A down vest was my dream, something to keep my body warm. But the good ones I had seen in a sporting goods store were way too expensive for me.

One night, as I joined Lee and other devotees in our late-night tea space, the Tavern, I noticed that he had a bunch of plastic bags beside him, obviously stuffed with clothing. When I found my place and sat down, he flashed a big smile, opened one of the nearby bags and pulled out a small bright-red down vest. "Is there anyone here who is small enough to fit into this?" he asked, glancing in my direction. Nobody else raised a hand, except me. Still grinning, he passed the prized item along to me.

In the Small Details

August 1994. A large crowd of sangha had gathered for dinner on a Tuesday night, one of two nights every week in which Lee prepared dinner for everyone. The greenhouse was packed with people eating and talking with enthusiasm. One of Lee's students sitting nearby him noticed that all the salads contained cheese. The young German man who was seated across from her was, she knew, on a strict regenerative diet and cheese was not allowed to him. Whenever he visited, Lee had instructed the cooks to fix something that this man could eat.

The woman who noticed asked Lee quietly, "Is there any salad without cheese? Anything for H.?"

Lee responded with characteristic candor, "Oh, I forgot." Then, he asked the young man to pass his plate to him. Receiving it, Lee began to take salad (without cheese!) off his own plate, generously piling it on for his devotee. Without a word of commentary, he smiled and returned the brimming plate to H., while he continued to eat his own slender portion with gusto.

The Kindest Touch

I was pregnant with my second child. Before leaving on a short trip, I walked into the greenhouse, our community gathering space, where Lee was seated on the floor, preoccupied on the phone with someone. Nonetheless, as I stepped into the room to say goodbye to him, but before I got a word out, he smiled at me and reached up his hand, taking my hand in his. Nothing more. Perfect.

"An Apology?!"

During my early years with Lee, I was feeling "ground through the mill," as they say. It seemed to me that I could never do anything right, could never please him. I spent a lot of those years crying, but also knew that much "work" was being done, on me and probably on some relationships with my previous life and the blood-family from which I came. Miraculously, I endured.

Then, many years later, after I had been living on the ashram and serving the sangha in numerous ways, I was in the kitchen during a talk that Lee was giving in the Darshan Hall. The talks were being recorded and were piped into the kitchen, so I could work and listen at the same time. To my utter amazement, Lee was talking about some remorse he felt about his way of being with some students. He expressed, in so many words, an apology to me and another woman for the hard line he had taken with us. Even though I was not in the room, I felt this apology like a shower of benediction. His love, after so many years of struggle for me, was unquestionable.

The Shirt Off My Back, Again

Lee often spoke of the need to act spontaneously, and frequently gave objective lessons of this sort. On one occasion, a group of us were eating in a nice Los Angeles restaurant. Lee was wearing a Mighty Mouse t-shirt. The hostess asked him where he got it, saying she'd like to give one to her boyfriend.

"You can have this one," Lee said, without hesitation. He then asked one of the men in our group to go out to the car and get him another shirt. When the man returned, Lee pulled off the Mighty Mouse tee, put on the new shirt and handed the prized one to the startled hostess. She thanked him and walked away from our table seemingly in a daze. Lee continued eating his dinner as if nothing unusual had happened.

Her Useless Club

I was playing Bridge at Lee's table one night. The bidding had resulted in the opponents' playing at four-spades. Early on in the bidding I had indicated the strength of my diamonds to my partner. When it was her turn to lead, she looked at her hand and hesitated, and then led a useless club. Much to my frustration, and based in her habit, she hadn't taken the cue to lead diamonds.

As I watched all the tricks get played and my fantastic diamond suite go to waste, I grew more and more annoyed at what I took to be my partner's willfulness and self-focus in not playing as part of a team. Just when my anger was reaching its peak, Lee looked over at me and said softly and gently, for my ears alone, "She doesn't understand."

He Would Feed Me

Upon arriving in Germany on a trip with the spiritual master, I was suffering greatly from back pain. One day, shortly after we got there, in an attempt to ease the pain, I was lying on the floor propped up by a pillow watching Lee play Bridge. Occasionally he would catch my eye and smile at me in a way that expressed the most tender regard.

As the dinner hour approached, Lee looked at me and remarked with a playful and loving tone, "Well, if you can't sit up for dinner, we will just have to have someone come and drop food into your mouth. We'll feed you."

You Get What You Need

Travelling in Germany with Lee, I had worried that I wouldn't get enough food to eat since it had been announced that we would only be having two meals a day. Breakfast at 10 a.m., and nothing else until 7:30 p.m. dinner. During morning meditation, the thought had flashed across my mind that perhaps I needed to create an excuse to go to town to buy myself a snack.

That night, during the late dinner meal, we were served a selection of goat cheeses, a present from one of Lee's French students. I ate hungrily, finding this cheese to be one of the most outstanding delicacies I had ever tasted.

The next morning at breakfast, as I sat at Lee's table, I happily remarked that the cheese from the previous night was probably the best I had ever had in my whole life. "Oh," Lee remarked, "that's wonderful!" Then he asked one of the servers if any cheese was left from the previous night's meal. Learning that a small amount still remained, he asked the man to get it and serve it to me. I was eating an apple at the time and Lee added happily, "It should go well with your apple."

I was touched profoundly. His individual care for each of us was beyond comprehension.

As I ate the cheese, he kept looking over at me and smiling, checking my progress. "Just eat as much as you can," he encouraged me. At one point, when I was licking my fingers with pleasure he said, "It's fantastic just to watch somebody enjoying something so much. It's like you can taste it too." I thanked him again and added that I was happy to give him the experience.

Here was the master again showing me that I could trust the abundance and the exquisite timing of his benediction.

Gracious Host, Gracious Guest

A couple from California visited the ashram to investigate Lee's teaching and to share the good company of other devotees. Our guests were strict vegetarians, and accustomed to a very pure diet, free of refined foods and sugar. They fully appreciated that junk food, sweets, and other items were generally not served on the ashram. During group meditation on the first day of their visit, however, they were surprised to see the devotees receiving candy out of a brass bowl. They knew that was *prasad* but asked, "If candy and all that stuff isn't allowed on the ashram, why does Lee give it to people?"

The story was passed on to Lee. "Wow," he said with a mischievous laugh, "next time they come up for prasad I should give them something *really* sweet, like two pounds of fudge."

The next day during darshan, however, when the guests came up for prasad, instead of receiving a wad of fudge, or even the customary candy, Lee gave them some peanuts.

The next afternoon when one of guests again approached for prasad, Lee asked him, "Would you rather have candy or peanuts?"

The man smiled broadly and, much to our surprise, enthusiastically asked for the candy! Lee smiled back and tossed the guy a small piece of imported chocolate.

All About Me

On one occasion, a group of us were busy in the ashram office when Lee finished reading a very long letter from a student. "I don't know why people bother to write me letters. They should just take a piece of paper and write ME on it in big letters and send that. Then I wouldn't have to plow through all this stuff!"

One of the men in the office who heard Lee's remark, said: "Wow, that would save me a lot of time on my monthly writeup for you."[36]

"Oh, you always think it's about *you* when I say stuff like that. You don't have to worry," Lee replied.

---

36 *Tariquat*, a series of questions that students in the early days used to update the master about their sadhana.

Simply Present

Years before I had moved onto the ashram, I returned home after a two-week visit in Arizona. As I walked into my house after a long plane ride and trip from the airport, I was tired but feeling so full from the visit. That's when the phone rang. It was the spiritual master.

He said, "Hello."

I said hello back, and then there was silence. I couldn't imagine why he had called. He didn't have anything to say and I didn't either, so I fell into the mood of simply being present to him, as one would be to a lover. Nothing *needed* to be said, and after a few minutes we just said goodbye.

My husband, also a devotee of Lee's, was in the room. "Who was that?" he asked.

"Lee," I said.

"What did he want?"

"Nothing," I replied. And that was that.

Gift of a Pin

I was visiting the Prescott ashram and meeting Lee for the first time. Several friends whom I trusted greatly had prepared me for the visit, and I was already impressed after only being there for a short time. One day, during that first Celebration, I was scheduled to give a performance in a local park downtown, and Lee and the whole community planned to attend. A bit nervous before I left for the show, I remember standing outside the ashram awaiting my ride when Lee walked up to me and asked, "Is there anything you need?"

The quality of his attention was so profound, so absolute, that I feel the effects of it to this day. There was nothing "there" except his pure presence and the simple and humble question, "Is there anything you need?"

In fact, I did need something—a safety pin to help fasten my costume. But to ask a spiritual teacher for a safety pin seemed out of the realm of what one would ever ask for in such a situation.

I hesitated for only a split second, but long enough to get that his question to me was completely unencumbered by anything else. It was so clear and so pure in some way that I was moved to tell the truth. "Yes," I told him, a bit embarrassed, "I need a safety pin."

He received my request with the same degree of complete openness and absolute attention and care with which he had asked the question. I could have asked him for anything, I think, and if I really needed it, he would have granted it.

"I'll be back in a minute," he said, as he turned back to the house. He returned a minute later and, without a word, placed a safety pin in my hand.

Receiving a Touch

I have the clear memory that I met Lee at the samadhi, Savitri (his tomb), soon after he died. My mom reminded me that she had brought me up to the ashram and we hung out at Savitri for a while. I am fifteen now, so I would have been only about two years old at the time.

All I know is that Lee put his hand on my back and spoke my name. This was real for me.

Sense of Humor

I was serving in our late-night tea gathering when another server put together an unusual variety of food for our guests. Lee came walking through the kitchen and stopped to look over the tray. "That's the most bizarre combination of food I've seen . . ." he said, as he took a few steps closer to the entrance to the space. Just as he left the kitchen he turned once more to finish his sentence, "since I was in Morocco 400 years ago." Then he smiled.

Nothing Special

I had traveled southwest on my way to the east coast when I stopped in Prescott, Arizona and stumbled upon the Mudra bookstore. What a goldmine! Spiritual books of every type. Wow. In conversation with the woman staffing the store, I learned about the presence of the nearby ashram, and she invited me to visit, which I did.

Following her there at the end of the day, and a few moments after I arrived, I saw "him," the guru she had told me about, in all his "nothing-specialness." Up close, however, I was most uncomfortable in facing him, as I had really nothing to say.

The next day, the group was going to a concert with Lee in Phoenix, and again I was invited to tag along. Imagine! They were going to see Fats Domino and Jerry Lee Lewis! Wonderful. I actually sat directly behind Lee throughout the evening production. Then, we all went out for hamburgers and fries…not my usual diet, but I loved it all.

I spent the night at the ashram and the next morning attended the morning practice, sitting in the meditation hall at the feet of the huge bodhisattva statue that graced the place. Lee was there too, and I let my eyes open to see him, at least at the end. Then I stumbled through the final chanting.

Overall, the intimacy of the whole encounter suited me. Nothing special, but everything very special. When I left the next day, Lee stood on the porch upstairs near the railing and waved goodbye to me.

For the rest of my trip I drove in silence, mostly. Couldn't really make sense of the experience but savored a growing appreciation for what I had encountered. I recollected the well-known rock lyric, "There's something happening here, what it is ain't exactly clear." [37]

[37] From the song, "For What It's Worth," by Buffalo Springfield.

In God's Good Time

One day, in a mood of great distress, and in tears, I went to Lee for help,

"When is this ever going to end," I questioned him, "these habitual patterns of speech and behavior that cause so much misery to myself and others?" I was hopeless.

Looking at me with great tenderness Lee replied, "It will end when it is no longer useful to God."

Who Are You?

I have always been struck by Lee's humility, which seems to be his natural state. He can be almost invisible, especially in his visits to other teachers or within a group he is attending where he doesn't want to be recognized as a spiritual teacher. Generally, he simply enters a room and sits at the back, and then leaves quietly. Occasionally, he is recognized, but somehow he always manages to remove the charge of that recognition and become invisible again.

One time, at a talk, another member of the audience began staring at him excitedly, and we knew he had been recognized. Just before the lecture began the man who apparently recognized him came over and addressed him, asking, "Aren't you Lee Lefkowitz?"

"No," said Lee, honestly, "I'm not."

"Oh," said the questioner, who then returned to his seat and paid no more attention to Lee.

The Bittersweet

At an after-dinner talk following our July 1985 Guru Purnima Celebration, I mentioned to the spiritual master about the sadness I felt when guests left.

"Don't be possessive," he said gently. "You will find that sadness becomes bittersweet."

Serving His Devotees

Late one Friday night, in our space of Tavern, the scheduled server did not show up. Consequently, the spiritual master took over the job of preparing tea, filling bowls with roasted nuts and arranging a plate of dates.

When I entered the space there was only one other woman present, so we sat together as Lee entered carrying two teacups on a silver tray. In our silence, and feeling both moved and discomforted, we accepted his offering, quietly whispered, "Thank you" and drank our tea as Lee exited back to the kitchen to fetch the nuts and dates.

This was a strangely wonderful, yet terrible, experience. To be served so directly was simply a reflection of how he served us with every gesture throughout the day and every day. I felt like what the Apostles must have felt when Jesus washed their feet at the Last Supper, like protesting, humbled, embarrassed. But it was obvious that the best means of thanking him would be to be a most gracious guest—to receive with open hearts what was being given and shown to us.

Too Many Coincidences

Initially, I saw Lee at a spiritual conference and didn't know much about him. I was at the conference to hear the work of another speaker. When I finally heard Lee's lecture, I didn't understand the language or the concepts he used to address spiritual work, so he didn't make much of an impression on me, or so I thought.

Returning home from the conference, I began reading the classic, *The Practice of the Presence of God* by Brother Lawrence, which I found profoundly moving in its simplicity and directness. Coincidentally, I later learned that this was one of the first books that Lee often recommended for his students to read.

Since I had seen Lee at the conference, I also ventured into reading some of his books, which I found to be powerful, but strangely didn't understand either. As time went on, however, I found that I couldn't stomach my previous diet of spiritual literature. I started leaving Lee's book, one with a picture of him on the back cover, standing up at the head of my bed.

About this same time, I started to do sitting meditation, to exercise regularly and to do some prayer practice without any idea that these were also basic practices that Lee had incorporated into the program for his students.

All of this happened for me as if in the dark, as I wasn't looking for a teacher. In fact, I thought I had a teacher already. But seven months later, I made my next contact with Lee and the school, and it took me a few more years before I engaged him as my teacher. It seems fortunate that the Process takes into account even the people, like me, who can't read the handwriting on the wall.

Nothing Doing

Late one night Lee remarked that students were declaring that he was a great devotee of his master, Yogi Ramsuratkumar. He exclaimed: "That's the most ridiculous thing I've ever heard! The fact is, I barely do anything…In fact, what I do is nothing, and Yogi Ramsuratkumar showers me with blessing."

Hearing these words, I playfully argued: "Well, Baba, that *is* the attitude of a devotee!"

Lee retorted: "Well, it might be, but I still did nothing!"

Too Expensive!

My husband and I were visiting the ashram from our home in New York City, and I was so excited to be visiting Lee again and experiencing his Sacred Bazaar for the first time. When we got there, I remember looking over the sacred objects for sale on the tables in the office, and being shocked to see how expensive they were. My partner and I were both working at the time, but our budget still was tight, especially considering where we lived.

The more I examined the pieces, the more I feel in love with them. A few times I saw a very small item that called to me, but when I showed it to my partner he would shake his head. No. We simply couldn't afford it.

Lee obviously noticed the play that was going on between us and made a special point of inviting us up to his room, where he had lots more bronze art and deities. We were surprised and so honored to receive his invitation that I was determined to buy something, no matter what!

Oh, the spectacle of his collections! It was enormous and glorious. One very small Ganesha caught my eye. It was perfect, I thought, and showed it to my husband before looking at the price. When he turned over the price tag both our faces dropped. This small beauty was way beyond our means.

With embarrassed gratitude we thanked Lee for the show and said that we would be considering our options. He smiled, gracious as ever, and we left the room. We left the ashram two days later having made no purchases. It was hard for both of us.

One year later, our New York group was hosting Lee and his family at a dinner we had prepared during his visit to the east coast. It was a formal affair, with fancy linens and tableware, and we all dressed up for the event. The hosts placed me and my husband directly opposite to Lee at the table for the meal, and again I was nervous and honored at the same time. Shortly after taking our places, Lee looked over at me directly and said, somewhat casually, "Oh, I almost forgot, I brought a present for you."

I didn't say anything, stunned as I was by his words. Then I watched as he reached into the breast pocket of his blue cotton dress shirt and removed a small object. Handing it to me discretely, he smiled. It was the same small Ganesha that I had longed for so many months ago.

By then I was crying.

Let Things Happen

Lee once said to me, "When you find yourself in the middle of a psychological turmoil do some crossword puzzles, and let things happen by themselves." I have seen him do that. I remember a time when an old family acquaintance of his visited him. She was particularly critical about some aspects of ashram life, and about his role as "a guru." On that day in particular, I walked into the living room and found him sitting with his feet on the coffee table. He was doing crossword puzzles for hours.

The Picnic

Living in Los Angeles where we were running a study group, my husband and I had been feeling an edginess together. One day, when the tension and despair became almost unbearable, my husband phoned Lee. They had a brief conversation and then he asked me if I wanted to talk too. I didn't. But a few minutes later, thinking the better of it, I phoned him back.

"Hi" Lee said warmly. He sounded relaxed and maybe slightly amused that I had called back. I told him how upset I was and he surprised me by saying that he did have a practical suggestion for us.

"Well, find a day when your husband doesn't have too many appointments and go on a picnic—just the two of you. "

I was momentarily stunned. Take a picnic? I hung up the phone and turned to my husband. "Do you know what he said," I asked. He stared at me blankly. "He said to take a picnic, just you and me!"

Early the next morning I went out for my daily mile run. As I headed down the block the piles of garbage at the curb reminded me it was trash day. I scanned the junk as I ran, looking for anything worth saving. Halfway along my route, I saw a wicker suitcase at the curb among several trash cans. I stopped to check it out. Whoever put the basket at the curb had wrapped a scarf around it that was tied in a bow on top, to hold it closed. It looked like a big present! I peered furtively over my shoulder at the house whose trash it was. Did they really mean to throw this away? Other than broken straps, it was in excellent condition. I loosened the bow of the scarf and pulled the case open on one side to peek in. Inside, I saw dishes and silverware—a complete and very elegant picnic set, circa 1925, with plastic plates, saucers, cups with tops, a set of drinking glasses, two plastic shot glasses, an old-fashioned thermos with a cork stopper, silver plated forks and spoons, shiny stainless-steel knives, and two plastic storage boxes with clip-on lids and metal carrying handles. Nothing was missing and everything appeared almost unused. The wicker case was itself lined with a pale-yellow fabric and had yellow straps to hold the contents in place. I closed the case and, as I retied the scarf around it, I suddenly noticed that it was made of a beautiful hand-dyed silk from India. I carried the basket home excitedly and called my husband to have a look at it.

As we stood admiring the case, it hit me for the first time: only yesterday afternoon Lee had told us to take a picnic. The coincidence was too uncanny. The more I thought about it, the more I marveled over the sequence of events.

A Miracle

In July 1988, we were attending a workshop by the author Jean Liedloff (author of the book, *Continuum Concept*). Halfway through the meeting Jean took a break and asked her secretary to go out to her car to get some additional copies of her books.

After an extended delay the secretary returned, red-faced, to announce that the key had become twisted in the lock and the car door would not open, and the key could not be removed. Jean was visibly upset, as she had no other key, and wondered how she would drive her car home. She then went outside herself to try to free the rogue key but also to no success and the resolution to call a locksmith.

Before she could make the call, however, Lee spoke up: "Let someone else give it a try," and quietly asked R. to have a look. "R. is really good at this sort of thing," he tried to assure Jean. But once again, after a few more minutes, R. returned to report that she too was unable to free the key from the lock. Disappointed, several of us then encouraged Jean to call the locksmith.

Before we realized it, Lee was on his feet and out the door. Jean, for her part, decided to wait out the result one more time. She began to speak to us about the subject of her work. Pausing to look out the window, she let out a gasp. "He's coming back," she said, "and he's got something in his hand." She sounded tentative, almost afraid.

Lee had only been gone for a minute or so. Could it really be true? A moment later we knew. Lee walked into the room smiling. He said nothing. Between his fingers he held the key which he handed to Jean.

[continued]

"I should have a man like you around all the time," she laughed, as did the rest of us.

"He's just doing what he does all the time with us," quipped a devotee.

What a Guy!

1984, a public darshan at the Unitarian Universalist Church in Boulder, Colorado. I remember being struck with how young Lee was. How funny and unpretentious. At one point, he unwrapped a whole wedge of brie cheese that had been offered to him as prasad, and proceeded to bite into it, seemingly prepared to eat the whole wedge like a sandwich. Then he put a jar of pickles (also offered as prasad) on the chair he had been sitting on and proceeded to get down on the floor and bow to it. The room erupted in laughter.

I didn't have any inclination to follow him, at the time, but I really liked the guy! He was quite the contrast to my previous experience in a spiritual community, especially with the formality of my years in the Catholic priesthood.

I was fifty-one at the time of this first meeting. Now, at eighty, I hope I am still a dedicated servant of this same guy, Lee, and the community I have lived within for over thirty-four years.

Guru's Grace

Lee died on Tuesday morning, November 16, 2010. The sangha was in the midst of a huge project—building Triveni Ashram in the high desert an hour's drive north of Prescott—as well as preparing for the annual celebration of Lee's birthday on November 18. Since Lee had not allowed anyone to talk about or plan for his death, everyone was suddenly plunged into a frenzy of tasks. Enormous decisions had to be made in the moment, on the run. In a state of raw awareness, we were thrown fully into the moment.

Lee's body lay in repose for two days at the old ashram in Prescott, then it was transported to Triveni, where it would rest for a third day in the large, two-story building that would be Lee's home. It was still under construction, an empty shell of beautiful potential, with rooms of unpainted sheetrock.

In the meantime, Lee's students, friends and guests were arriving from Europe, Canada, Mexico and all around the U.S. One hundred and thirty people began to gather for the traditional Hindu ceremony that would occur in the afternoon on November 19. Lee's friends Arnaud and Veronique Desjardins, Eric and Sophie Edelmann, Rob Schmidt and Stuart Goodnick from California, and Dr. Robert Svoboda arrived. Robert had provided the most auspicious day and time, according to Jyotish astrology, for the final interment of Lee's body—around five p.m. on Sunday, November 21.

Devotees from the U.S. and Europe labored hard with hammers and saws to complete a simple wood-frame roof to cover the heavy granite sarcophagus until the samadhi *mandir* (temple) could be built—a project that would take years. Many people worked long hours to orchestrate and manage all that was needed for this supreme moment—our guru's transition from this world to the next. Hearts soared with ecstasy and sheer joy even as tears were shed in the bittersweet finality of his death.

When the sun dawned on November 21, the rainbows began to appear. One of the carpenters working onsite saw the first one at 7:30. All day long the sky was adorned and we watched in wonder. Clouds came and went with icy snow flurries, rain, and bright sun in between. Devotees driving out from Prescott for the interment of Lee's body watched in awe as rainbow after rainbow came and went in arcs across the sky. Even the locals in the grocery store line were chatting excitedly—they'd never seen so many rainbows at one time!

"I stopped counting at twenty-five," said the carpenter. There were over a hundred rainbows that day, seen as far away as the road from Mingus Mountain, sixty miles distant.

Student to Teacher

Student: "I don't understand Lee."

Arnaud Desjardins: "Ah, but you should know him better since you have been on a band tour with him."

Veronique Desjardins: "We love Lee for many different reasons, but he is eminently mysterious, and un-understandable."

Arnaud: "Yes, every authentic spiritual master is in some particular way mysterious and un-understandable."

CODA

In his Journals, and occasionally in passing or during one of his talks, Lee gave us a few epitaphs for his gravestone. A few remembered ones:

If I die today just write "He Made Us Laugh" on my gravestone.

—source unknown

Today, and until further notice, when I die I would like on my Samadhi/Tombstone/Vase or whatever the following:

"He was a little too human."—May 14, 1990[38]

OK. If I were to die today,
I would like my tombstone to read:

"Don't take it personally."
—March 7, 1994[39]

ॐ

[38] Mr. Lee Khépa Baul, *The Eccentricities, Idiosyncrasies, And Sacred Utterances Of A Contemporary Western Baul,* Prescott, Arizona: Hohm Press, 1991, p.27

[39] Mr. Lee Khépa Baul, *In the Mood of, In the Style of, the Eccentricities, Idiosyncrasies, And Sacred Utterances Of A Contemporary Western Baul,* Prescott, Arizona: Hohm Press, 1994, p.158

And on March 13, 2009,[40] he expressed how he would like to be remembered:

> I would like to be remembered by my children in the same way that I remember my father, Louis Lozowick, and I don't feel that is at all mundane or irrelevant to my "profession" or to the context in which that question might be posed in a "spiritual" interview. And secondly…I'd like to be remembered for what I left behind, the vast resources of dharma in all forms of Objective Art that I support and that I and my students are producing: writing, both prose and poetry…painting, sculpture and the moving arts, martial as well as other forms; and in the living lineage, a body of students who truly embody the Transparency that is the Blessing of the lineage, that could also be languaged as "the acceptance of what is, as it is, here and now," or "Just This," my teaching of Assertion, and the integration of that into a profound Transmission of Truth, Reality and Objective Sanity, to all and anyone, and furthermore who embody vast skillful means and cellular kindness, generosity and compassion. Yes, I think that says it.

---

40 lee lozowick, (Noted Subject), *Chasing Your Tail: Notes That May Be Difficult to Follow On Subjects That May Be Difficult to Grasp*, Prescott, Arizona: Hohm Press, 2009, p. 89

AFTERWORD

by Rick Lewis

With Lee, you never knew what was coming.

It was a bitterly cold day in Montreal, but the landscape was luminous under the snow-reflected sun. So much light was coming through the windows that my retinas were aching trying to withstand the radiance.

I was a new student, attending a multi-day seminar with Lee in Quebec, Canada, where he was guest teaching at a meditation center established by the late spiritual teacher, Arnaud Desjardins. Each conference day featured three teaching sessions of two hours each. We were in the middle of day four, outside the meeting room on a break, standing behind a folding table that was filled with books. Lee was selling them.

The blinding sunshine filled that hallway where a line-up of attendees waited to get personal book recommendations from Lee. He loved both books and sales with irrepressible enthusiasm. Traveling with numerous boxes of trade books to sell at events, authored by himself as well as other credible guides, was a routine he relished.

I was assisting him at the table, working invisibly as a runner—helping to locate specific books within stacks on the table, or on my hands and knees rifling through boxes below to locate study material he'd occasionally recommend to a practitioner. I was entranced with the way Lee moved—with an economy and elegance that seemed to demonstrate exactly the way hands should unwrap a book, a friendly smile ought to be delivered, or a signature ought to be spilled onto a page.

This was a new and intriguing world to me. My own relationship to inner development had always been a wordless process. I was drawn to meditation and especially the aesthetic of Zen, which had led to my dismissal of books and words in favor of silence. I'd abandoned reading, writing, and the mental clutter of language in favor of the pure pursuit of ineffable inner space. Now I had a teacher who was fond of saying, "If it's not written down, it didn't happen." Lee's commitment to communicating complex and nuanced principles about human development and the spiritual path in precise and artful words was fundamental to his teaching work, and he expected his students to embrace it.

I, on the other hand, had spent the last few decades becoming a competent, successful, and *silent*, physical comedian. I had mastered sufficient circus skills, comedic timing, and command of a crowd to earn my living as a performer. I enjoyed a sense of authority in front of an audience without the anxiety of having to grapple with language.

That was about to change.

The buying queue at the book table had slowly dwindled down to the last few who wanted to get personal recommendations for study material. Eventually, the last person stepped forward and stood facing Lee. She half-opened her mouth, presumably to introduce herself, but before she could utter a word, he said something inexplicably strange that neither I, nor the woman, had any idea how to parse.

I was bent over rearranging boxes behind the table, the bridge of my nose level with its edge. My teacher's oddly emphatic words to this woman as he gestured toward me—scooting around on dusty knees—were, "This is *Rick Lewis*—author of many books!"

I looked up at him, confused. The woman looked down at me, perplexed.

He had introduced me like I was Isaac bloody Asimov, undiscovered, and now he was rectifying the unjust obscurity. But why the heck had he introduced me at *all*?

I hadn't written *anything*—other than a few personal letters to him. Me. The same person who was arrogantly consumed with the idea that words were a waste to time and beneath my spiritual stature.

He didn't explain or elaborate, to me or to the woman, but simply resumed the social exchange, sold her a book, and expected me to retrieve it—despite the identity vertigo that was now disorienting my brain.

Today, many years after Lee's death, I've indeed authored a few books. And the practice of writing has unquestionably opened the door to life experiences—personal, professional, and spiritual—that have been of incalculable value to me.

But the point of this story is that my teacher saw a potential for me that I did not recognize at the time. His comment seeded a capacity I had yet to discover. His words were simple, but his tone carried exuberant praise. Praise he offered without any visible proof. He was using his speech to appreciate something that did not yet exist. I might even say he was authoring *me*, guiding me toward an essential story I was here to enact.

I saw him do this for many individuals over the years. Businesses were created, ashrams built, performances delivered, songs composed, art produced, books penned, and children raised that simply would have never appeared without Lee's suggestion that they were destined to be. He demonstrated praise as an invocational force of human expression that not only affirms the existence of what is manifest, but also manifests what has the potential to exist.

Lee could appear to be crazy-wise, cutting, and wield a vajra sword with unparalleled skill and ferocity, and yet, to me, the essence of Lee Lozowick was praise. Brilliant, shining, radiant praise. A quality of praise that could level one's individual army of doubts in an instant. He used praise as a means of extending affection, providing affirmation, and acknowledging affinity. And his praise often took the form of humor, where he would tease the delicious ironies, idiosyncrasies, and eccentricities of human life out of the shadows and render workable even what we considered to be our personal horrors.

I could say a lot more about Lee. An accomplished and enthusiastic salesman, bookstore owner, bridge player, champion of children and conscious parenting, prolific poet, lyricist, a father himself, and most importantly, true heart-son of his Master, Yogi Ramsuratkumar.

I could talk about how he insisted on wearing open sandals in the dead of winter and had a half-buried car in his front yard. How I'd personally seen him dismantle the defenses of the most hardened characters in public and fortify the strength and self-esteem of those in need of functional stability.

How I watched him ruthlessly dress-down the unconscious habits of established students and then beam at them with an adoring gaze. And how the mood around him was unpredictable, exciting, and a little dangerous.

But all of that was secondary to the ever-shining light of his presence as a force of praise. He was an unqualified invitation to simply exist.

A fellow student recently asked me what I thought Lee had left behind. What was his legacy, or primary contribution to his generation of spiritual seekers and practitioners?

I thought about the dozens of books that Lee himself had authored. The thousands of hours of talks he gave that today sit in an archive of audio and video recordings that were captured by his students. Lee spoke at length on every spiritual tradition under the sun, what we could learn from Sufism, Buddhism, Christianity, Hinduism, and Zen teachings. He read voraciously, studying the work of historic spiritual masters, and sharing their insights with his own added commentary. He was constantly visiting contemporary teachers, soaking up perspectives, opening himself to feedback, and offering assistance when it was requested. I thought of the hundreds of songs he wrote, the bands he started, the many tours in which he performed.

And yet, none of that was the reason for the trailing line of people waiting to experience a minute with him at the book table. The reason for the queue, and the reason students regularly flew around the world to sit and play cards with him at his ashram, was best expressed by Lee's close spiritual peer Arnaud Desjardins. He said, "Nobody is more like himself, than Lee."

Perhaps that doesn't seem like a great feat. But I'd suggest it's because this is a truly rare demonstration of humanness. Lee ruined many of us this way. By being himself. Because you couldn't experience a demonstration of authenticity like that and walk away without suddenly knowing that you, and most of the humans you've ever met, have been faking it. And once you've seen the real thing, you must either devote the rest of your life to the pursuit of naturalness, or you'll have to double-down on the lie. And the lie is easier. As Miles Davis once said, "Sometimes you have to play a long time to play like yourself."

The flesh and blood authenticity that was demonstrated by Lee is, I believe, his enduring legacy. This *being himself*—offering the warmth of his presence—again and again, was like throwing a hundred thousand pebbles into the pond of human experience. That influence has rippled its way into more moments of intimacy, connection, self-honesty, clarity, generosity, kindness, and compassion among real people than we could ever know.

Today Lee's presence remains so palpable to me that I can't honestly say I miss him in spirit—who he really was—because that radiance still *is*. But that doesn't mean I wouldn't pay dearly for a chance to stand side by side with Lee the man as a happy accomplice to his theft of hearts at a book table again. The memory of watching him work his magic in that bare hallway on that day is one I will forever cherish.

Perhaps because all that light wasn't just coming through the windows.

ABOUT HOHM PRESS

Hohm Press is committed to publishing books that provide readers with alternatives to the materialistic values of the current culture, and promote self-awareness, the recognition of interdependence, and compassion. Our subject areas include parenting, transpersonal psychology, religious studies, women's studies, the arts and poetry.

Contact Information: Hohm Press, PO Box 4410, Chino Valley, Arizona, 86323, USA; 800-381-2700, or 928-636-3331; email: publisher@hohmpress.com

Visit our website at www.hohmpress.com